14.99

ABOUTFACE

ABOUTFACE

CELEBRITY MAKEUP TECHNIQUES **SCOTT BARNES**

Foreword by Jennifer Lopez

First published in the UK in 2010 by
Apple Press
7 Greenland Street
London NW1 0ND
United Kingdom
www.apple-press.com

© **2010 by Fair Winds Press**

ISBN: 978-1-84543-350-5

10 9 8 7 6 5 4 3 2

Cover and book design by Alisha Neumaier
Book layout by Carol Holtz
Photography by Karl Simone

PRINTED AND BOUND IN CHINA

In memory
    of my brother,
John Barnes.

What wine is so sparkling, so fragrant, so intoxicating as **POSSIBILITY.**
—Kierkegaard

contents

foreword

It was springtime or summer of 2000 or 2001. I can't remember exactly, but I do remember the sun was shining. It was a beautiful day. I was doing a photo shoot for *In Style* magazine in downtown Manhattan, and I was trying out a new makeup artist, which can always be interesting...

I walked over to the hair and makeup table and a guy with a big smile and a head full of cherubic, light brown curls held out his hand to me and said, "Hi, I'm Scott," and I immediately felt at home. I don't know if it was the warmth of his smile or the easy, comfortable way about him, but I knew it was going to be a special day!

I sat down in the chair and immediately Scott went to work. He said, "I am all about skin, and yours is gorgeous. We are gonna make you glow!!" Well, I didn't realize the half of it. His lovely, positive attitude and personality were only a precursor to his talent, which can be described as nothing short of makeup magic. He had a special touch. Long story short, he has been making me "glow" ever since!

That same day I told him I had another photo shoot and a video shoot coming up for my new album, *J.Lo*, and I told him, "I want you to do it." We started talking about ideas and realized we had a lot in common. One thing we shared was that we both love glamour and anything glamourous, and since that sunny afternoon we have created a countless number of glamourous moments together. And that's where it was born: a relationship that continues to this day.

One of the many blessings of working in this business is getting to work with other artists who have a passion for what they do. From that passion, they are able to change the future and create what's new and what's modern—what's today. This is the kind of talent Scott has. He's a true artist. He wants everyone to be beautiful and feel beautiful inside and out, and he has always made me feel that way when I am sitting in his chair: that I am the most beautiful woman in the world (and trust me: that is no easy task on a movie set at 5:30 in the morning).

Like any relationship that spans years we have been through so much together: ups and downs, ins and outs. We have worked through disagreements, breakups, marriages, divorces, and even deaths, growing closer through it all as true friends do. I am honoured to have been able to work with this man who I believe to be the best makeup artist in the business today. But I am even more honoured to call him my dear, dear friend. I hope you enjoy this book and all of its helpful information and little secrets, many of which he has used on this face, too!!

Have an absolutely beautiful time! I know you will.

St. Regis Hotel, New York City, 2004.

Photograph by Marc Anthony.

introduction

Transformation

It's a powerful concept, especially when it comes to your appearance. And *About Face* is about the ability to transform your look from average to extraordinary. Makeup can certainly work to transform a person. It can help a woman feel more confident, sexy, and beautiful. But this book isn't just about makeup techniques. It's about learning how to accept yourself and enhance what you've got. You have to feel good about yourself before you can begin to feel beautiful. You've heard the old cliché, "Beauty starts from within." Like it or not, ladies, it's a true statement.

Most of us look in the mirror and focus on what we wish we could change. My forehead is too high, my lips are too thin, or my cheeks are too fat...the list goes on. But what if you looked in the mirror and focused on the fact that all these things you don't like about yourself are the very things that make you you? That's your uniqueness, what sets you apart. Finding your beauty isn't about looking exactly like everyone else. It's about accepting yourself—the parts you love and the parts you don't—and then working with all of it.

When I look at women I find each and every one of them beautiful. Because each and every woman is distinct. The combination of face shape, features, and smile: that's what makes a woman beautiful. All the women in this book started out gorgeous in their own way, and I simply gave them new ways to emphasize their unparalleled look. So, as you read about the various makeup techniques I present here and check out the transformations, take a look at yourself in the mirror and remind yourself that, among the millions of women out there, there's no one quite like you. Be gentle with yourself. Love yourself. Embrace the beauty of "you." Once you've done that, you're ready to start playing with the power of makeup to transform yourself into anything you want to be, including your most beautiful, most exceptional self.

About Face contains beauty rituals I've perfected over my years of working with many models and celebrities, as well as expert advice from my team of trusted consultants. You'll find portraits, step-by-step guides, and interviews with many women describing their own beauty regimens and transformations. You can use this information to affect your own transformation, capitalizing on

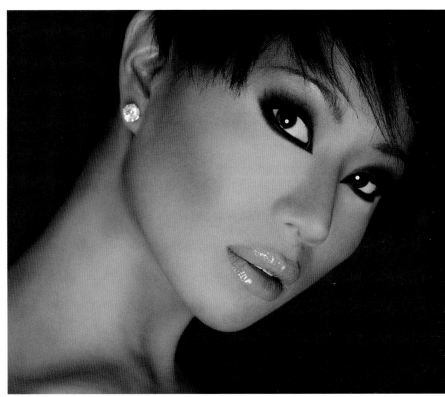

your distinct features to create a look that's unequaled. I want all women, not just my clients, to feel beautiful and empowered. Feeling beautiful leads to self-respect. Self-respect leads to greater confidence. And confidence commands attention. So, let's begin your journey to becoming your most beautiful, most exceptional self.

THE GLAM SQUAD

Karl Simone (PHOTORAPHY)

I was born and raised in Toronto. I first picked up a camera in high school art class, fell in love with it, and never really put it down. I have always found it necessary to be creative. It's just something that comes naturally to me, and I am so appreciative that I get to do something creative for a living. I met Scott in Miami in the early 1990s, and he and I immediately hit it off. We both share a love for creating something beautiful and have been talking about shooting a book together for a while. I am extremely proud of what we have created, our collaboration on these images, and our friendship.

They say "Beauty is in the eye of the beholder," but as I've learned through my experience as a photographer, it is also in the beholder of the camera.

The camera is a very strange instrument. It allows people to take on a new identity. It's about photographing not only those who are beautiful but also those who feel beautiful. Creating an "illusion" of beauty begins with a process. Makeup, hair, clothing, and lighting—each is an essential ingredient, but they are not as important as a woman's sense of self. These women were on a journey that took them to another level of self-awareness that translated on both sides of the lens. Each is unique in personality, yet they all share the same desire to feel great about who they are as women.

Watching Scott transform them, I saw their faces change both physically and emotionally. It was amazing and inspiring to witness, to say the least. As each woman stepped in front of the camera, I was able to capture a new-found confidence and beauty. This was, indeed, a transformational experience for each and every one of them. After all, it is about face.

Chuck Amos (HAIR)

I love working with hair and making women feel beautiful. You must feel beautiful to be beautiful. If you really like a particular look, even if other people say it looks crazy on you, that's what you should go for. Because it shines through who you are, you feel comfortable and great. Being beautiful on the outside is really just an enhancement to what you can feel on the inside. There's no real standard of beauty. I think it's different for each person.

I never want to overtake my clients' look by giving them over-the-top hair if they feel uncomfortable about it; yet, I want to give the world something they've never seen in hair before. I see myself more as a hair artist/illusionist than a hairstylist because my learning journey on the subject has been from every aspect. So, now I can do or make just about anything with hair, from major sculptures to organizing fashion show hair for twenty-five models. There is nothing I cannot do with hair at this point, and I love the adventure of it. The passion for it overtakes the feeling of work, so it's easy to put all my heart into my work. I've touched the heads of Diana Ross, Donna Summer, En Vogue, Beyoncé, Destiny's Child, Vanessa Williams, Tyra Banks, Naomi Campbell, Lauren Hutton, Ivana Trump, Jewel... the list goes on. In addition to working with many wonderful celebrities, some of the highlights of my career include doing a Versace show in South Africa (and meeting Nelson Mandela) and being the first African American to do the hair for the cover of *Paris Vogue*.

Ultimately, I like to consider myself an illusionist instead of a hairstylist since I do all sorts of tricks with hair that no one usually sees. (I was doing extensions when they were considered faux pas!) Scott is the face and body illusionist; he showed me how the illusion of makeup can really work with the illusion of hair. The end result is true genius.

Jocelyn Goldstein
(WARDROBE)

Styling in particular is something I sort of fell into, and I have had the good fortune of working with and learning from some of the best people in the industry for the past ten years. I started as an intern at Isaac Mizrahi and then moved on to an internship with the fashion director at *Vibe* magazine. It was there that I discovered that my favourite part of the job was going on shoots. So, I began working as an assistant on different editorial and ad campaigns, with my first job being on a Burberry ad campaign in Paris. I also assisted Camilla Nickerson, an editor at *Vogue* magazine, who has now moved on to *W* magazine. I continued assisting various stylists, including Andrea Lieberman, doing lots of video and print work, as well as red carpet work. Andrea continues to be a great mentor and friend. Now, I work solo on various commercial, celeb, and editorial shoots. The job itself never gets old. I still have butterflies when I work, as there is always a new challenge to face.

When Scott Barnes does makeup, it's amazing to see how expressive, yet effortless, his art can be. When we work together we are inspired by one another and work to create beautiful images. But although we can work hard to get the most amazing hair, makeup, and clothing on a person, if the beauty doesn't also come from within, it's useless.

Sometimes people have the tendency to put on everything they love all at once. But it's not necessarily about that. Fashion is so individual. It's a feeling you get when you see somebody wearing something that looks amazing, and you think, "Oh my God; that works!" Sometimes the process of dressing a model is organic, but sometimes it isn't. Ultimately, it's about trying different clothes, experimenting, and making sure the outfit makes the person look and feel beautiful. If you have confidence, you can look beautiful because you know you are beautiful.

The Power of BEAUTY

We've always been fascinated with stories of transformation. Some of the most beautiful and memorable females in history and literature are women who have gone through significant transformations. There's Eliza Doolittle, the low-class flower girl turned high-class lady in George Bernard Shaw's play, Pygmalion, who later sang her way into people's hearts in the popular musical, My Fair Lady. The Cinderella story about the ill-treated sister who becomes a princess is known by children the world over. Even Gigi, the Academy Award–winning movie musical based on the French novel of the same title, portrays an awkward teenager being groomed as a courtesan who evolves into a respectable young woman. These stories serve as wonderful morality tales about the implications of physical transformation. But in my mind, the most powerful transformation is the one found in the Bible's Book of Esther. It's the original transformation story, and I think it best depicts the power of beauty.

Esther is a young Jewish peasant girl who is ultimately selected to become the wife of the Persian king, Ahasuerus (some texts refer to him as King Xerxes). Esther uses her beauty to find favour with the king and become his queen. But the story doesn't stop there. As queen, Esther, along with her cousin Mordecai, is able to persuade the king to cancel an order for the extermination of Jews in his kingdom. Today, the Jewish festival of Purim celebrates this event.

Keep in mind that this girl was the daughter of a goat herder. Being a peasant, she was probably very dirty. She didn't wear fine clothes or jewelry, and it's doubtful she had time to comb and set her hair. So, there was definitely some grooming involved before she presented herself to the king. What's remarkable about Esther is that she could've easily viewed her success at finding favour with the king as an impossible feat. After all, the odds were certainly against her. She was a girl from humble means whose parents had died and whose faith conflicted with that of the king. Instead of giving up, though, she did what she needed to do to make herself as beautiful as possible to get the king's attention. She had an open, positive approach and saw the opportunity presented to her.

Esther made a conscious effort to be better. She actively sought the king's favour, and in so doing, she actively sought God's favour.

This story, as with the other transformation stories mentioned earlier, is not just about beauty for vanity's sake. These tales show how each woman effects change in the lives of people around them. Esther's story is the most significant in that her beauty saved the Jews from being massacred. It doesn't get more significant than saving a race of people. Her beauty led to her living a purpose-driven life. Although the king noticed Esther because of her outer beauty, it was her inner beauty, her strength of character, and her actions that influenced a positive outcome. Even in the stories of Cinderella, My Fair Lady, and Gigi, the women are more than just pretty faces. They impress others with their nobility of character. These are women of substance who because they come from more humble beginnings have a generosity of spirit, a compassion for others, and a humility that intensifies their beauty. There's grace in humility. Humility is downright sexy.

The women chosen for this book are certainly beautiful women. But as you read their stories, you will see that they are also women of substance. Something more than vanity drives them to take care of themselves. They are passionate about such things as photography, privacy, animals, and family. They are women who believe in taking care of their bodies and stimulating their minds, and they believe they have something to offer the world. Their physical transformations only help to bolster these beliefs.

One last thing: The best part about the stories of Esther, Cinderella, Eliza, and Gigi is that each of these women also finally realized she was no less important or no less worthy than the other "beautiful" people around her. Each woman gained confidence and self-worth in the process of her own transformation. It's an important point. In fact, it may even be the point: If you're doing things to make yourself feel better and look better—grooming yourself, eating well, exercising, and doing whatever it takes to become your most beautiful self—it can benefit you in extraordinary ways that stretch far beyond mere physical appearance. I think of it as empowering yourself, having a spiritual relationship with *Self*. And that's the real power of beauty.

You have the power
to create your own
MASTERPIECE.
—Scott Barnes

The Scott Barnes
APPROACH

Before you jump into these transformations, there's something you should know: the way I approach makeup application is very different than the way most people approach it. I think in terms of light, so I first begin by looking at a face, seeing where the light hits it, and then working with highlighting and contouring to bring about "a glow." This approach allows the features on the face to stand out and gives a woman that "lit from within" look. Most people, by contrast, do contouring and highlighting after most of the makeup is already applied.

Also, I don't necessarily put makeup on in the same order. I'll always begin with contouring and highlighting; but then for one model I might put on blush before eye shadow, and then for another model I might do it the other way around. It all depends on what I'm seeing at the time and the look I'm creating for that particular woman. Each face is unique; each application is a work of its own.

Another thing people sometimes find surprising is that I use brushes for applying just about every kind of makeup—from eye shadow and blush to concealer and foundation, no matter whether they're in powder, cream, or liquid form. This is simply because I've found brushes to offer the best control and smoothest blending. Period.

Before each of these transformations, I applied a hydrating mask and gave each woman a mini-facial massage with a lymphatic drain to moisturize and relax the face. Moisturizing is an important step towards smooth makeup application since makeup adheres better to moist, supple skin than it does dry, flaky skin. You can use a light moisturizer for everyday application and then opt for a hydrating mask when getting ready for special occasions. Removing facial tension is an equally important step for achieving a relaxed, confident look.

My hope is that some of these new approaches will excite you enough to try them for yourself. If you're confused about anything, just turn to the "Breaking It Down" section in the middle of this book. That's where I've tried to anticipate your questions, cover the essentials, and provide the reasons for a particular technique; most likely the answer you're seeking is there. You'll also find various tips scattered throughout the book for saving time, money, and frustration when approaching your own beauty regimen.

The most important thing to remember is that there are no hard and fast rules when it comes to makeup application. So, I encourage you to be bold, have fun, and experiment. Dare to surprise yourself with the results. Your willingness to break out of old patterns means you're well on your way toward realizing a whole new you.

I used both red and yellow foundations to stay as close as possible to the light and dark of her NATURAL COLOURING.

Transformations

1

Katherine:
How to Make Glamour Work

Katherine Albrecht is a well-known privacy expert. She got her doctorate in education from Harvard, she's the author of the bestselling book *Spychips*, and she hosts the syndicated US radio show "Uncovering the Truth." As a freedom campaigner, she's far from the typical angry activist who doesn't know how to present herself. In fact, she's just the opposite. Katherine knows her power as a woman, and with her transformation, she's learned how she can take her femininity even further when fighting for an important cause. Now when people meet her for the first time, they're surprised by just how beautiful, how confident, and even how sexy she is. What a great way to start any conversation, even if it's with your adversary.

Scott + Katherine Talk ...

SCOTT: What is your beauty regime in the morning?

KATHERINE: It depends on whether I'm going out into the world or whether I'm working in my home office. Typically, even if I'm working from home, I will wash my face with a washcloth and water. Pretty straightforward, nothing fancy. I have really dry skin, especially in the wintertime, so my biggest problem is not to remove oil; it's what's keeping my skin moisturized.

SCOTT: Right, water's actually better for your skin than soap, because water leaves some of your natural oils behind. It's like leaving natural oils in your hair.

KATHERINE: Yes, exactly. And when I do use a cleanser, usually when I need to remove a lot of makeup, I try to use really rich, creamy cleansers. Then I follow that up with a moisturizer. For makeup, I typically put on just a little bit of foundation, because I kind of need it. My skin's a little blotchy and freckly,

(continued on page 35)

Creating Katherine's Look

1a

1b

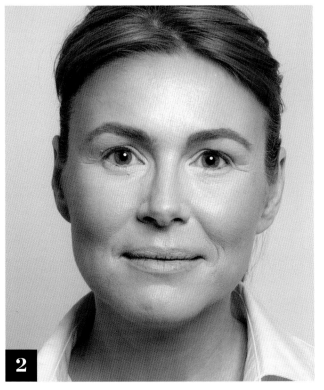

2

Tip To find the apples of your cheeks...simply smile.

Katherine told me the thing she struggled with most was her eyes. She knew they were small, but she felt that eye makeup made them look even smaller. Her eyes are a great colour—a pale gray-blue-green—so I set out to show her how she could get more wow power with them.

....

1 Contouring, highlighting, and foundation

Katherine has a healthy complexion with a lot of red undertones. I wanted to alleviate some of the redness in her skin by using a pinky-beige colour for her foundation and give her a more unified tone overall. **(a)** Using light strokes with a goat hair brush, I applied a cream contouring (dark) foundation: ● Underneath the jaw line ● Underneath the cheekbones ● On the sides of the nose ● At the temples ● Under the tip of the nose (to give the illusion of shortening the nose) **(b)** Using a goat hair concealer brush, I applied a cream highlighting (light) concealer: ● On top of the cheekbones ● In the centre of the forehead ● Under the eyes ● Underneath the eyebrows ● On the bridge of the nose ● At the centre of the chin **(c)** Using a third goat hair brush, I applied a cream pinky-beige foundation on top of the contouring and highlighting and blended by moving the brush in a circular motion for a smooth, seamless transition.

2 Cheeks

I used a coral blush that matched her natural lip tone and applied the blush on the apples of her cheeks, moving the blush brush in small circles.

Tip Katherine has red hair. In addition to matching her natural lip tone, coral is also good on a redhead because it has a lot of yellow in it which complements red hair; however, it still has enough pink in it so that the effect isn't muddy-looking.

(continued from page 33)

so I put on just a little bit of a very light, light foundation. I usually follow that with a little lipstick, a dash of eye shadow, a little mascara, and I'm good to go.

SCOTT: How would you define "beautiful"?
KATHERINE: I think "beautiful" is silky, glowing hair glowing skin, healthy skin, and overall good health. If you don't feel healthy, it shows, even with all the makeup in the world. There's a difference in your posture and everything else about you when you feel good. There's an element of sexy in beauty, too. It's that feminine thing that so many of us forget to project as we become busy with other things, especially those of us who have been married a long time. But I think if you really want to have the va-voom kind of beauty, there's an element of sexy that you need to put back into your beauty regimen.

SCOTT: Do you think a person can be smart and sexy?
KATHERINE: Absolutely, I think they totally go hand in hand. For the past ten years my job as an activist has been to intimidate men specifically. Ninety percent of the people I deal with

(continued on page 37)

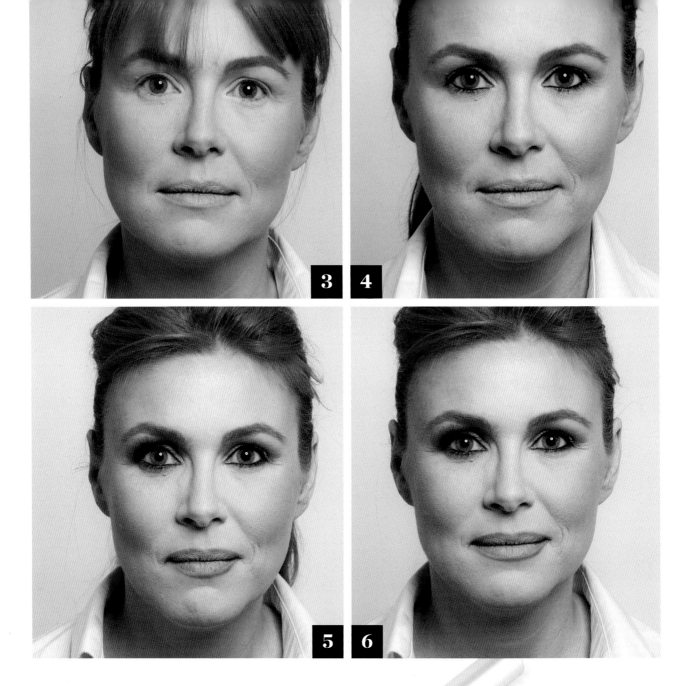

Tip For eyelashes that stay curled, hold down the eyelash curler for a count of 20 and then apply mascara immediately.

Tip For redheads, lining the eyelid with a brown pencil helps bring out the eyes, while still being a softer, more natural look than lining with a black pencil.

3 Eyebrows

Katherine's eyebrows were in pretty good shape, so I trimmed them only minimally to clean them up. I also filled them in with a mustard-coloured eye shadow using an angled brow brush. Katherine has brown eyebrows, so I put yellow shadow on them to bring out more red in her eyebrows to compliment her red hair since the combination of brown and yellow makes red!

4 Eyes

Most redheads have light eyes, and Katherine is no exception. Her eyes are a beautiful pale gray-blue-green, which deserve to be highlighted. **(a)** For the eye shadow base, I selected a colour two shades darker than her hair—a reddish brown colour—and brushed it over the whole eye. **(b)** Then with a different eye shadow brush, I applied a darker chocolate brown shadow into the crease, under the eye, on the top of the lid by the lash line. **(c)** I then lined the inside rim of her eye with a chocolate brown pencil. Note: Katherine could easily switch out this brown liner for black liner to create a more dramatic look for special events. **(d)** Finally, I curled her eyelashes and applied lots of black mascara, which provides more drama than brown mascara. The end result is a much fuller, thicker, bolder eye that doesn't look too harsh or heavily made up since I used brown-toned eye shadow and liner instead of Katherine's typical black eyeliner look.

5 Lips

Redheads have a tendency to go red-brown with their lipstick, which I think is a mistake. The darker colour draws focus away from the eyes and clashes with the hair. It's usually better to go with a lighter-coloured lipstick instead of a darker colour to avoid the lip colour overpowering the rest of your lighter features, particularly your eyes. **(a)** I lined Katherine's lips with a pale auburn liner to draw her hair colour back into her face. **(b)** I then applied a pale coral gloss since I didn't want to make the whole lip auburn.

6 Setting the look

I finished off with a nice dusting of translucent powder so as not to change the colour of the foundation and the blush. Using a large powder brush, I lightly swept the powder all over her face and neck for an even finish.

(continued from page 35)

are men, and they're some of the most powerful corporate executives in the world. I think a smart and powerful woman can be intimidating to men, but I think femininity in general—being a powerful, sexy woman—can be even more intimidating.

SCOTT: Do you think it's important to be beautiful in your line of work?
KATHERINE: I think a woman can be extremely smart and competent, but when she adds that extra layer of "beauty," it's as if people are able to see her competence more quickly.

REACTIONS...

Katherine's Reaction to Her Transformation

"I've learned that there's a little bit of an extra edge that comes from being a beautiful, strong, powerful woman, particularly when you're having an open debate with men. Breaking down the stereotype of the mean, ugly, negative, angry female activist is a part of my power. I love the fact that Scott has helped me to break through that activist stereotype even more with a new look, especially since I believe that looking and feeling my best helps attract more people to the cause. Who wants to follow an angry, ugly person? People would much rather follow somebody who's positive and who feels really good about herself."

"Before, I was the confident, professional businesswoman, but now I also have the ability to be over-the-top glamourous, if I choose. And people treat you very differently when you possess both qualities. In fact, just the other day, I had to travel to Los Angeles for a meeting, and I had literally forgotten to pack my makeup in my suitcase, so I had nothing to put on except pale pink lipstick. Here I was with my glasses on and my pale pink lipstick and my hair pulled back in a ponytail, and it was so funny because the guy I met told me how great my photo was on my website. But his subtext was...'and you're not really that pretty in person.' So, I went out during our lunch break, bought £50 worth of makeup, sat in my car, and did the whole Scott Barnes makeover and then went back to the meeting. That same guy

and everybody else around him treated me like I was a different person. You can tell, it's like night and day... a different level of appreciation and admiration that people treat you with when you do the whole Scott Barnes makeup thing. They treat you like you're more competent, like you are more 'deserving' of their respect. I didn't feel disrespected before, but there's definitely a feeling that you're one of the people in charge of the situation, instead of one of the people in the background."

Gate:
Combining Earth Tones for a Monochromatic Look

There's a long-standing debate about whether Egypt was settled by Africans or Europeans. Gate, a model, is Ethiopian. She made a point of telling me this when I remarked that her bone structure and features reminded me of the ancient Egyptians. She went on to explain that Ethiopia is "mixed" and consists of people from many different parts of the world—Africa, India, Egypt, Italy, Yemen, and Israel—and that her parents are black Ethiopians. I did a bit of research and discovered that Ethiopians—and Somalis in particular—are said to most closely resemble the ancient Egyptians and Nubians. Some sociologists believe, in fact, that Egyptians are actually descendents of Ethiopians who migrated into Egypt. That fits with my perception of Gate as an Egyptian princess. Perhaps it has more to do with the regal way she carries herself. Or maybe it's because her actions are also stately. Her husband, who is the chef for the five-star restaurant, Aquavit, introduced Gate to UNICEF. Now, in addition to modelling, she works with UNICEF on Africa–U.S. relations. Gate is a beautiful woman with an admirable nobility of character, and she deserves a look that's equally distinguished.

Scott + Gate Talk ...

SCOTT: What is your typical diet?
GATE: I'm not really picky, but I know what I like. I love food, but I don't really eat junk food. I'm married to a chef, so I eat very healthy food everyday. He cooks, and teaches me things. So even when he's not home, I make myself a nice chicken dish or fish dish or a salad. I like lamb...soft meat...not cow meat. I like to eat, so I exercise almost every day.

SCOTT: What kind of exercise do you do?
GATE: I take a West African dance class. I also do yoga, play basketball, and go biking. I also walk a lot every day, which is also a good workout.

SCOTT: Do you wear a lot of makeup usually?
GATE: No, I wear no makeup when I'm not working. I just want my skin fresh. I used to wear a lot of makeup, but my skin was getting irritated by using a lot of different products. So, when I'm not working, I just wear mascara and lip gloss, so I can let my skin rest from having to wear makeup.

(continued on page 43)

Creating Gate's Look

Tip Women with dark skin should have two or three foundations that they can blend on the face to create a more natural-looking foundation with greater dimension. Dark skin is never one colour; usually it has two or three tones. So, when applying foundation you want to try to mimic the natural colouring of these different tones. Otherwise, you risk flattening out the face and making it either too light or too dark overall using only one colour.

(continued from page 41)

Although Gate's darker colouring would have allowed using more colour on her face, I decided to go for a simpler, more monochromatic look for her since she wasn't used to seeing herself made up that way. Therefore, I used colours in the warm brown and gold family for Gate.

1 Eyebrows

I started with Gate's eyebrows. I wanted to take off the sharp points at the arches to give a more feminine softness to her look **(a)** Using a razor comb, I trimmed the point off her arches to create a rounder shape. (You can jump to "Breaking It Down" to learn more about the razor comb technique for trimming eyebrows.) **(b)** I then plucked a few remaining stragglers with tweezers.

3 Cheeks

Using a blush brush, I blended a cream burgundy blush on the apples of Gate's cheeks, moving the brush in a circular motion. You can never go wrong with burgundy—a terrific blush colour for darker skin.

2 Contouring, highlighting, and foundation

Gate's skin contains both red and yellow pigment, so that she has both lighter and darker areas on her face. The combination of these two colours gave Gate an overall bronzy skin tone. When applying foundation, I wanted to be sure I didn't flatten out her face by using only one colour of foundation. For that reason, I used both red and yellow foundations to stay as close as possible to the light and dark of her natural colouring. **(a)** With light brush strokes, I used a goat hair brush to apply a cream reddish-burgundy contouring foundation: ● At the top of the forehead where the hairline meets the skin ● Underneath the cheekbones ● On the sides of the nose ● At the inner eye where the bridge of the nose meets the brow bone ● At the jaw line **(b)** Using a goat hair concealer brush, I applied a cream yellow highlighting concealer: ● Underneath the eyes ● On top of the cheekbones ● From the forehead down the bridge of the nose ● In the centre of the chin **(c)** Using a third goat hair brush, I applied a thin layer of golden brown cream foundation on top of the contoured and highlighted areas and blended, moving the brush in a circular motion for a smoother effect, while still creating depth and dimension.

SCOTT: What is your first memory of using makeup?
GATE: I've always liked makeup, but I was always afraid to use it because my brother was a priest. I grew up with him in Holland. So, on my way to school, I would put on makeup on the train, and then I'd take it off on my way home because I couldn't look different. My brother never told me not to use makeup, but I felt that I shouldn't wear it around him in order to show respect for his work. But I knew I looked great with makeup!

I also remember my first shoot as a model for The London Times. They put makeup on me, and I was like, "Oh my god, I look really, really nice!" After that, I couldn't wait until a makeup artist touched my face!

4 Setting the look

This is a very important step for setting the foundation and blush and creating a flawless finish. **(a)** Using a large fluffy powder brush, I dusted a light tan loose powder with yellow undertones all over Gate's face and neck. **(b)** I then tapped the excess powder from the brush onto a powder puff. I folded the puff as though making a taco and smushed the powder into the puff to bury the excess powder into the puff. I gently dabbed the puff against the skin to set the makeup.

5 Lips

Since I had opted for a monochromatic look for Gate, I kept her lip colour a warm brown shade, instead of going with something more pink. **(a)** I used a brown lip liner (which was actually a brown eyebrow pencil) and followed her natural lip line. **(b)** I filled in with a tinted lip gloss called Smoky Topaz. It looks like hot chocolate, but it goes on much more sheer.

6 Eyes

This wasn't about building an eyelid, as much as it was about accentuating Gate's almond-shaped eyes. To give the illusion of larger eyes, I elongated the length of Gate's eyes in both directions. **(a)** Using a black eyeliner pencil, I rimmed the whole eye, top and bottom, and extended the inner corner and outercorner of the eye. **(b)** I swept a loose shimmer eye shadow with a green undertone over the whole eyelid. **(c)** I finished off with lots of black mascara and opted not to use false eyelashes to keep the look simple and clean.

REACTIONS...

Gate's Reaction to Her Transformation

"I was like...wow! I looked and felt totally different! Scott didn't put a lot of makeup on my face, but he knew about my colouring and just what I needed. Many makeup artists use so much more makeup."

"I've tried all kinds of makeup before. I've been in the modelling industry for five years, and I haven't found one foundation that I really love. Because of my dark skin, I need yellows and reds. And the way he applied my foundation was perfect for my skin. And the concealer he used looks amazing. It evens out my skin and goes on so easily."

Kat DeLuna ★

Since she's such an
AUTHENTIC TALENT,
I wanted to see
Kat with a look that
was more unique,
something she
could really own.

Scott on Kat

Kat describes herself as an up-and-coming artist, and I predict it won't be long before the rest of the world catches on to her talent. She's the real thing—not just another marketing package—with all the right stuff to become a huge success. Being classically trained in opera, Kat can sing like a bird. Or she can do down-and-dirty pop. This girl's got range, with a voice that'll knock your socks off. And have you seen her dance?! To watch her move, you'd never guess she was never formally trained.

Since she's such an authentic talent, I wanted to see Kat with a look that was more unique, something she could really own. Kat is from the Dominican Republic, so I encouraged her to drop the blonde look and go back to her natural colouring. Her Latin roots are very important to her, so she liked the idea of going with a style that supports who she is and what she believes in. Her fan base keeps growing, so it seems they've embraced the new Kat. There's a lot that's special about this bilingual singer-songwriter, and I look forward to watching her wind ...all the way to the top.

Kat on Being a Singer-Songwriter, Scott, and Finding the Beauty Within

I've been singing ever since I can remember. The first time I ever performed was in a talent contest in the Dominican Republic. I was three years old, and I sang a very powerful Spanish ballad. All the judges wondered how this three-year-old girl could sing such a song. I ended up winning the contest, and that's how it all started. My mom and dad have always been very supportive of me. They are very musical themselves, but they were never able to explore their talent, primarily because of economic pressures. So, I guess in a way I'm living their dream.

I've always written my own music. I wrote or co-wrote my first album and also produced and vocal-produced it. My music is more than art to me; it's an inspiration of life. That's why you'll hear a lot of happy tunes by me, like "Whine Up," my first single. I also try to decorate my music with a little bit of opera because I'm a classically trained singer.

And I love to dance. Being from the Dominican Republic, my whole family always danced—a lot. So, I learned how to wind as a child, dancing at parties. I especially love to mambo—love it!

My dream is to win some Grammys and become an iconic figure in the world of music. But I would like to win because of my music, not because of other things. Hopefully I can be a role model, not only for children, but for many people around the world who might find inspiration in seeing me—a young girl who came from nothing—make something of myself. I would like to use my success to help others somehow. Music, fashion, makeup, or the movies—anything artistic has a way of connecting people. It's a way of uniting people peacefully.

I was so honoured when Scott chose me to be one of the women in this book. He stands out from a lot of other makeup artists because he's an artist first, and not someone who simply applies makeup. I've seen him do other people's makeup and I've seen him do my makeup, and it's like he's creating a piece of art. He knows how to adorn each of his clients in a certain way that brings out what's unique in them. Like when I first broke into the music industry, I dyed my hair blonde. It was cool for a time, but I started to see that with my hair blonde, a lot of colours that I used with my natural dark hair didn't work with blonde hair. When I met Scott, he encouraged me to go back to my roots, and he completely changed my look for the better. He's also been so generous with me. Whenever he does my makeup, he teaches me a lot in the process.

The fact that Scott's involved creatively in his makeup line is a major plus. His house is like a lab, and Scott's like a makeup scientist who crafts his makeup—literally makes his own colours—specifically for the person he's working with. He'll be like, "Let me see what colour is beautiful for you." In that way he's more of an innovator. He will be remembered for his work, not because he works on celebrities but because he has found a way to make a woman feel beautiful about herself.

And that's the key: to find the beauty within yourself. There's a beautiful woman inside each of us; it doesn't matter what age we are. And we're all made differently for a reason. Just like flowers; every single flower is beautiful, no matter what family it comes from. God made it so we could adore each one of them for their own unique-ness. And that's how I feel about women. Women often try to imitate each other or try to look a certain way because they think that's what society wants. But I feel we should work with the tools God has given us, what we were born with. Every woman has her flaws, so we have to learn how to love our flaws and work with them, to see them as our beauty marks—like my freckles. I had to learn to love my freckles, and now I think they are the most beautiful part of my body.

So, always look for the beauty within yourself, and then you'll figure out how to bring it out. Also remember: Life is only lived once, so I say live it and have some fun!

Louisa:
A Low-Maintenance Approach to Achieving High Drama

Scott + Louisa Talk ...

Louisa likes competition. As a kid, she competed in high jump, relay races, and volleyball. She also grew up around horses. She participated in "jumper" competitions and did every kind of riding, from cross country to stadium. Today Louisa still competes: as a model, as a marathon runner, and as a jumper with her thoroughbred mix mare, Bellini. So, it makes sense that Louisa sports a short, almost boyish hairstyle that doesn't require a lot of maintenance.

A hairstyle can often dictate a person's look, and in Louisa's case, her short hair, in combination with her tall, non-curvy physique, tends to give her a rather androgynous appearance when she's not wearing any makeup. Instead of fighting it, I decided to go further in that direction. I took inspiration from one of our most captivating andro supermodels of all time: Twiggy. Keeping in mind Louisa's low-maintenance approach to beauty, I wanted to dramatically change her look without taking a lot of time to get there. Louisa learned that sometimes, with only a few small changes, the difference can be striking.

SCOTT: When did you cut your hair short?

LOUISA: When I was in high school, I competed as a high jumper. And I actually won most of my meets. But at one point my ponytail started hitting the bar, so I left practice that day, headed straight to the salon, and got it whacked off. I was a little competitive, and I thought, "If this is what it takes...." I even had a personal trainer at the time, so I guess I was pretty serious about it.

SCOTT: Do you ever miss having long hair?

LOUISA: No, I love my short hair! I have a petite face and super-thick hair, so when it was long, it was a little overwhelming. Now, it's easier to deal with and I can sometimes get away with leaving it messy. For modelling work, the shorter hair is great since most other models have longer hair. So, it makes me stand out since they can spike up my hair or slick it back for a different look.

(continued on page 55)

Creating Louisa's Look

1

2

3a

3b

3c

Louisa doesn't want to spend a lot of time on her makeup. And when you have good skin, you don't have to. While Louisa usually prefers a more natural, no-makeup look most of the time, she still wants the option of creating a look with more impact for special occasions. I showed her how simple it is to create more drama with just a few small changes, while still keeping an appearance that is more natural and fresh.

....

1 Highlighting

I left Louisa's skin tone alone and didn't do any contouring or concealing. I worked only with highlighter and let her natural skin tone—which was slightly darker than the highlighter—supply the darker shading. **(a)** With light feathery strokes, I applied a cream highlighting concealer using a goat hair highlighter brush: ● On top of the cheekbones ● On the brow bone ● Underneath the eyes ● On the bridge of the nose Since Louisa's skin was in such good condition and I was going for the most time-efficient makeover, I applied no foundation.

2 Cheeks

Louisa also had prominent cheekbones, so I could get away with applying a minimal amount of makeup for a more natural, no-makeup look. **(a)** Using a shimmer highlight, I applied a light dusting on the top of Louisa's cheekbones, just enough to make them "pop." **(b)** I applied a rose-coloured cream blush and blended in a circulation motion to give a healthy glow to her cheeks without adding a lot of colour, since the rose tint was very close to Louisa's natural colouring.

3 Eyes

Louisa has deep-set eyes, so I wanted to bring them out. But I didn't want to spend a lot of time applying shadow, so I decided to stay away from adding any kind of coloured eye shadow altogether. **(a)** I added a heavy false eyelash on the top lids. You can see how simply adding false eyelashes can go a long way toward creating a more dramatic effect. **(b)** I added a strip of false lashes underneath her eye as well for even more drama than mascara only would provide. Note that it's easiest to apply a lash under the eye if you adhere the lash to the centre of the eye first, then press on the outer corner, and finally the inner corner. **(c)** I then lined the inner rim of Louisa's eyes with a dark brown Maybelline pencil, after softening it to create a softer, charcoal effect. Since I was using false eyelashes on Louisa, I wanted to be sure to line all the way to the inner corner and connect on the inner corner with the liner, so the lining didn't stop short at the end of the false eyelashes.

(continued from page 53)

SCOTT: How much time do you typically allow for makeup?
LOUISA: Not much. I've never been the type to wear a lot of makeup. In fact, I remember in high school, when prom came up, I had no idea how to do makeup. So, I bought the Kevin Aucoin makeup book, and I tried to follow his techniques. I also remember he had a section about pulling back the skin with tape for a kind of temporary face-lift. I wanted to try it on my grandmother because, of course, she had so many wrinkles. So, I literally taped her up with Scotch tape and thought, "Why is it not looking the same?" I still can't believe she let me do that.

SCOTT: It sounds like you do a lot in the way of exercise.
LOUISA: Every day. I'm an early riser—I usually get up around 6 or 6:30—and I work out first. I like to either get out for a run or go to the gym. I enjoy really long runs, six miles or more. I like doing a lot of half marathons and shorter races here and there, and I'm also working toward a full marathon.

(continued on page 57)

Remember, half of feeling good
is looking good,
and looking good leads
to **FEELING GOOD.**

4 Lips

Louisa has a very pretty mouth with a beautiful smile and great teeth. To keep it natural, I didn't want to change anything on her lips by lining them with a colour that was darker or lighter than their natural colour. I simply wanted to enhance her lips. **(a)** Following her natural lip line, I lined the lips with a beige-peach colour to match her natural lip colour. **(b)** I finished off with some sheer lip gloss to complete Louisa's look.

I accomplished Louisa's transformation in less than thirty minutes. It's a great example of how you can still make a bold statement without spending hours doing your makeup.

4

How to Soften a Maybelline Pencil

Simply take a cigarette lighter and wave the pencil through the flame a couple of times to soften it. When the tip gets clumpy, it's at the right temperature (still slightly warm), and you can use it like a crayon for a charcoal-like effect. You can always draw on your hand first if you're worried that it might be too hot. It will look more like coal. Not only does this technique provide a soft lining effect, but also the makeup cools down inside your eye, which means it stays put once applied.

Important: Remember to blow on the pencil to cool it down some before putting it on your eye! You can always draw on your hand first if you're worried that it might be too hot.

(continued from page 55)

SCOTT: What do you do to take care of your skin?
LOUISA: I always wear sunscreen during the day. I've got two: SPF 15 and SPF 25. I'm big on switching up products, so I'll go back and forth between brands. I hear some women say they use the same product for forty years. But I feel like you can get different things from different products since they're all made up of different ingredients, so I like to switch it up.

After I wash my face with a mild cleanser, I'll put on moisturizer and eye cream—always eye cream. At night, I almost always wash my face, but sometimes I'll get a little lazy. If I have makeup on, I'll definitely wash or if I've been running around the city all day because I usually feel like I have slime on my face. Then I'll moisturize with a night cream, but without any SPF, and more eye cream.

(continued on page 58)

REACTIONS...

(continued from page 57)

SCOTT: Do you have any kind of philosophy when it comes to beauty?

LOUISA: Do everything in moderation—even moderation. I think life is meant to be enjoyed. There's always so much "do this, don't do that" and "eat this, don't eat that." I think it should be about maintaining a well-balanced approach. When people who know me see me drinking coffee, they think "that's a little hypocritical" because I'm always talking about nutrition. But I'm pretty healthy overall, so my one espresso in the morning isn't going to shut me down. I can go without the coffee, but it makes me happy, so I feel it's okay to allow myself such things as long as I do it in moderation.

SCOTT: Do you have any plans once you're no longer modelling?

LOUISA: On the weekends, I'm in nutrition school. I'm already working toward becoming a holistic health counselor. I've got a website and a few clients rolling in already! That's my new focus lately, which in addition to everything else is keeping me super busy.

Louisa's Reaction to Her Transformation

"I look great! Compared to other makeup artists Scott took a 'less is more' approach. Everything looks fairly natural but has such impact. The whole process was super simple. For starters, Scott didn't cake on the foundation or powder like most makeup artists do. And he totally worked my eyes. He explained to me that my eyes are a little deep-set, so some extra liner and some lashes will go a long way to make them pop. And it's so true. I definitely work the liner more now. I don't wear a lot of makeup unless I'm going out, but when I do, I now know I can focus on the eyes and lashes."

Jessica:
Creating a Believable Faux Tan for Face and Body

Jessica's dream is to become a freelance artist. As a studio art major at New York University, Jessica balances her time between a full course load at NYU and a part-time modelling career. At nineteen years old, she comes across as a highly disciplined, extremely pragmatic individual. She's already focusing on landing an internship, stating that "as fun as it would be to be an artist showing my work in galleries, it's kind of dicey to try to make a living doing only that." So, she's decided to explore the art direction and media side of the art world as her backup plan.

Jessica has terrifically blue eyes, but her skin tone is more golden than that of a typical Caucasian, so I asked about her nationality. She told me she was a mix between Irish, Scottish, German, and a bit of Cherokee Indian and that she gets "really dark in the summer." Perfect. I could easily picture her on a beach somewhere in the Caribbean. But I wanted to show her how she could get that same deep tan without spending so much time in the sun, damaging her skin. Bronze goddess, here we come.

Scott + Jessica Talk ...

SCOTT: What do you think are your best features?
JESSICA: I always thought my eyes were probably my best feature—and my hair.

SCOTT: You have lots of hair.
JESSICA: I know, and I never, ever brush it, which is probably not good, but I have a sensitive scalp; besides, I kind of like the messier look, it's more me. I'm a natural, very low-key girl when it comes to styling. If I'm going out, I'll blow out my hair and then throw on some product to give it some volume, scrunch, and go. Or I'll just throw my hair up in a bun. I'm also low-key with my makeup. If I do wear makeup, it's very light. I usually wear very subtle eye shadow, if I wear any at all, like a light brown or something in an earth tone. I'll also throw on mascara, which is pretty much my staple—and lip gloss.

(continued on page 63)

Creating, Jessica's Look

Tip Remember to blend until all the colours are married together, for a smooth finish with no separation of colours.

(continued from page 61)

Jessica seemed pleased when she talked about getting really tan in the summer. I don't blame her—everybody feels better with a bit of colour. Fortunately for her, she has some Cherokee in her, so her skin tans easily without burning. Still, we all know how damaging those ultra violet rays can be and how quickly skin ages when overexposed to the sun. So, it was important to show Jessica how she could create a faux tan and feel just as beautiful as if it were the real thing.

1 Contouring, highlighting, and foundation

For Jessica, it was about creating a unilateral tan all over her body that required minimal contouring and highlighting. **(a)** I started with Jessica's body and applied Body Bling all over to fake a tan. The trick with applying Body Bling, as with applying any kind of makeup, is—you guessed it—blending thoroughly! Keep smoothing it into your skin so that it mixes with your natural oils and so that you don't end up with darker patches anywhere. **(b)** Once her body was sufficiently bronzed, I moved on to her face. Jessica felt her nose was "too wide," so I showed her how to slim it with contouring. Using a goat hair brush, I applied contouring (dark) foundation: ● On both sides of Jessica's nose **(c)** I used bronze cream foundation that matched the bronze of her body and applied it with a goat hair brush all over her face, moving the large brush in a circular motion. **(d)** Using a smaller highlighter brush, I dusted Shimmer Highlight: ● On top of the cheekbones ● On the forehead

2 Cheeks

I applied a reddish-tan cream blush to the apples of her cheeks, blending in small circles. I chose that colour to mimic a sun-kissed look.

(continued on page 65)

Even though the colours
I used are very similar to
one another, they still ideally
require **SEPARATE BRUSHES**
for application.

3a

3b

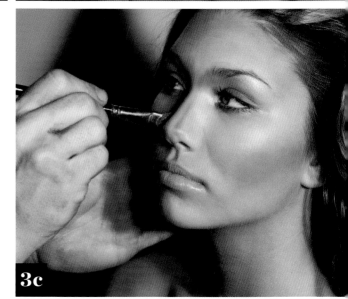

3c

(continued from page 63)

SCOTT: Sounds like you're doing all the right things. How about eating habits?

JESSICA: I was raised on a vegetarian diet. I'll eat red meat every once in a while, but I've always stayed away from chicken. But I love fish. My mom used to cook white fish or tuna or swordfish. But since I've been living at NYU, I eat dorm food.

SCOTT: How's that going?

JESSICA: Let's just say I miss my mom's cooking.

3 Eyes

The goal was to keep the look as natural as possible, so I avoided applying a lot of colour and lining to Jessica's eyes. Even though the colours I used are very similar to one another, they still ideally require separate brushes for application. If you don't have separate brushes, just be sure to wipe the excess colour off your brush before moving on to the next colour. **(a)** I lined the lower rim of her eyes with a golden-peachy eye shadow to bring out the blue in Jessica's eyes. **(b)** I applied copper eye shadow all over her upper eyelids—from brow to lash, inside to outside corner. **(c)** I lined the lower eyelids with auburn eyeliner pencil. I used a colour with a reddish tint that would appear as if she had no makeup on but would still help to accentuate her blue eyes.

4 Lips

I completed the look by adding sheer lip gloss. Jessica already had nice full lips, so no lip liner was necessary for this all-natural look.

REACTIONS...

Jessica's Reaction to Her Transformation

"I look like I just came off the beach!"

"It's crazy, because I've never seen myself look quite like this with makeup. It's really amazing what can be done with makeup to change the way your whole face and body look. It's like plastic surgery without the surgery. I'm so impressed. And it's good to finally learn how to apply bronzer. Scott showed me that it's all about blending and making everything even. It's nice to know that I can achieve this look without spending a lot of time in the sun."

"I really do feel beautiful—like a bronze goddess. And it's only makeup! That's just crazy."

scott barnes

**BODY
BLING**
PLATINUM

MOISTURIZING
SHIMMERING
BODY LOTION

LOTION HYDRATANTE
HÂLEE POUR LE CORPS

120 ml ℮ / 4 fl. oz.

scott barnes

**BODY
BLING**
PLATINUM

MOISTURIZING
SHIMMERING
BODY LOTION

LOTION HYDRATANTE
HÂLEE POUR LE CORPS

scott barnes

**BODY
BLING**
ORIGINAL

MOISTURIZING
SHIMMERING
BODY LOTION

LOTION HYDRATANTE
HÂLEE POUR LE CORPS

scott barnes

**BODY
BLING**
ORIGINAL

MOISTURIZING
SHIMMERING
BODY LOTION

LOTION HYDRATANTE
HÂLEE POUR LE CORPS

120 ml ℮ / 4 fl. oz.

Scott Barnes on Self-Tanning

There are several faux tanning techniques, including self-tanners or bronzers. I created Body Bling™ as an alternative to the sun for immediate results. Self-tanners take a few hours to develop, and sometime have an unpleasant odor. Whether using self-tanners or bronzers, alone or in combination, the results are stunning and saves your skin. Here are some tips to glow like a pro.

FACE

The biggest no-no when applying self-tanner to the face is putting too much lotion underneath your eyes, in the creases of your nose or mouth, or anyplace where, if you go darker, it will age you, such as in the creases of your skin. You want to try to create a halo around the face with the tanning solution, while keeping those areas in the centre of your face a little lighter.

BODY

It's really important to cover your nails and palms with rubber gloves. Roll the gloves down below your wrist in such a way that you keep your palms covered but most of the top of your hand is exposed. Rub the solution all over your body, and when you're finished, take the gloves off and rub the remaining lotion toward the ends of your fingers. This keeps the colour minimal on your hands so that you avoid creating darker "monkey knuckles."

Also remember to cover your toenails (Scotch tape or Band-Aids work well). This ensures that you don't get yellow toenails or cuticles.

There's always the challenge of reaching your back. The easiest solution is to invite a friend over to help you. Have your own little tanning party: a "you tan my back, I'll tan yours" kind of thing. You can also try using a tanning spray, which sometimes helps you reach the centre of your back a little more easily.

If you do make a mistake, such as making your elbows or your knees too dark, don't panic. Use Veet or some such hair removal product, which removes tanning colour like it removes hair, only faster. Apply it for 30 seconds or less and then wipe away.

Mariska Hargitay ★

Scott on Mariska

Mariska is an award-winning actress. She's also the president and founder of the Joyful Heart Foundation, an organization dedicated to providing support and encouragement to survivors of sexual assault. Joyful Heart is an apt name since I think Mariska is a most joyful, generous woman. With her megawatt smile, she's exudes a sense of warmth and confidence that give her real presence. But perhaps the most appealing thing about Mariska and what many people don't know about her is that *she is really funny!* She's got a killer sense of humor, which reveals itself through her constant stream of humorous anecdotes and her impeccable comic timing. Whenever I work with Mariska, I always know it's going to be a day of fun and laughter. As talented as she is in *Law & Order: Special Victim's Unit*, I keep hoping she gets more chances to do comedy. She actually appeared in a sitcom, *Can't Hurry Love*, for a short time, but I think the world has yet to discover Mariska the comedian. Maybe I should say stunt comedian, because Mariska is also fearless to the point of insisting she do all her own stunts on *Law & Order* (much to the chagrin of her producers). She could probably do one hell of a pratfall and have us all in stitches! There's simply nothing shy or girly-girl about this gifted, versatile actress. Her courage, strength, and uplifting spirit have allowed Mariska to touch many lives, both on camera as a tough but empathetic New York City detective and off camera as a compassionate leader who endeavors to heal wounded souls. It just doesn't get any more beautiful than that.

> Whenever I work with Mariska, I always know it's going to be a day of fun and LAUGHTER.

Mariska on Scott and Her "Secrets" for Staying Beautiful

I met Scott about three years ago on a cover shoot for *Redbook*. When I sat down in Scott's chair, I thought, "Wow, here I am with this guy who everyone says is the best, who is amazing, and who works on all of these fabulous movie stars." So, he worked on me for a couple of minutes, and then I looked up and saw stripes of makeup on my face...stripes... three distinct stripes. And I thought, "Oh no, I'm in the wrong chair, I look like a tiger, and I belong in a zoo..." Almost as if sensing my fear, Scott said, "Hold on, I'm not finished." And he continued to work his magic. Moments later, he finished blending my makeup in a way I had never seen before. It was radiant and incredibly natural-looking. I felt absolutely trans-formed and more beautiful than I could have ever imagined. After that experience, I became one of Scott's biggest fans. I've never seen anyone work the way Scott does. His techniques are innovative, and his appli-cations are unique. And he is versatile. One time he makes me look like a glamourous movie star, and the next time he gives

me a natural, sun-kissed feeling, like I just stepped off a beach in Tahiti—and I always look about ten years younger. I also love his energy, and I trust him implicitly. Bottom line: When I'm working with Scott, I know I'm in the presence of a true artist.

I think that women today receive both positive and negative messages when it comes to what it means to be beautiful. Some people are trying to spread a positive message when they talk about embracing yourself for who you are and not judging yourself according to the numbers on the scale. But there's no question that there are other voices out there pressuring women to hold themselves to impossible standards. As women, we just have to focus on the positive voices and make sure they're louder than the negative ones. For instance, I have a zigzag scar on my forehead. Most people think of scars as imperfections, things they want to remove or erase. And I used to feel that way about my scar. But now I like it, because I know it's unique

to me. It's all mine. It kind of makes me feel like Harry Potter. It gives me strength.

I think it's important to feel good about yourself. Here are a few of my secrets on looking and feeling my best—or at least some things I do to help me keep it more or less together in the midst of all the craziness:
● No matter how busy you get, make time to care for yourself. Some TLC for the mind, body, and spirit is a must. Set aside an hour a week for your own mini "spa day." If you can't manage an hour, do what you can. (And don't spend the time beating yourself up about how you don't make enough time for yourself. TLC, remember?) Take a warm bath, light a beautiful candle, or paint your toenails purple. A little indulgence goes a long way. ● Wear clothes that look and feel good to you. Forget the trends. Focus on colours and cuts that send your confidence soaring. Believe me, everybody looks good wearing a little confidence. ● Hydrate. Give yourself more of what you're made of. Our bodies are mostly water, so we need

to replenish physically, just as much as we need to replenish spiritually and mentally. Plus, it'll be great for your skin.

● Eat well. This is an absolute must. I'm not saying you need to lunch at a five-star restaurant every day (especially in today's economy). It's about getting a balanced diet; you know the drill. For me, it's also about a little extra dark chocolate. They call it "the healthy chocolate." Seriously—a girl's gotta leave room for chocolate, right?! ● Listen to your body. Make sure you're finding the right balance of work, exercise, rest, and play. Your body will tell you what it needs; it's up to you to listen. But if it's saying, "Let's sit on the couch all day watching TV," tell it: "After we go the gym." ● Get in touch with your creative self. Start a journal, paint a picture, or grab your camera and take a walk. The best part is that you don't have to show it to anybody. Creative expression feeds your spirit, not some person looking over your shoulder, telling you to paint faster. ● Breathe. Take a moment, close your eyes, and just focus on your breath-

ing. In the midst of all the chaos, there's a calm, centred, healthy, joyful self in there that may just need a little air. ● Laugh. There's just nothing better for the soul. ● Finally, find your passion. Whether it's hang-gliding, antique books, karate, or volunteering your time... anything! I'm passionate about the Joyful Heart Foundation. It's an organization I started in 2004 to help survivors of sexual assault, domestic violence, and child abuse heal and reclaim their lives. Since then, more than 2,000 survivors have participated in our pioneering retreat and wellness programs. We reach thousands more with information on our website, and our participation in national educational and media awareness campaigns has planted the seeds of change in the lives of millions. But Joyful Heart isn't about affecting millions on a day-to-day basis. It's about touching the heart of the individual, one person at a time. I have seen the light go on again inside so many survivors. And it's those beautifully miraculous moments that keep me going in this work.

The work we do, the hearts we open, and the incredible people we encounter along the way—these are the roots of inspiration for me. So, find something for yourself that makes your heart joyful. That's how you make the most difference. And making a difference can lead to feeling good about who you are. It can give you confidence.

Confidence is beautiful. Compassion is beautiful. To have both with grace is beautiful. A person is beautiful when she has the courage to embrace her own potential and make choices for her life that are in sync with what's in her heart. And there's almost no bad hair day that a big smile and a little mascara can't fix! Although I do admit that there are those mornings when I wake up, look in the mirror, and think, "Man, I wish Scott Barnes were here to work his magic."

Nadiya:
Achieving That Sultry Look

Nadiya is a long way from her roots. She's originally from Donick City, a small industrial town in the Ukraine that exports coal. She works full time as a print model and in TV commercials, but like the rest of the women in this book, Nadiya is more than just a pretty face. Having already seen much of the world, she has aspirations of moving into politics to help make a difference to those less fortunate in other parts of the world. She regularly volunteers her time at a local soup kitchen which she finds "inspiring" and that has given her a new appreciation for her own life.

When Nadiya walked into the studio, she immediately evoked the image of an Italian film siren—the kind of confident woman who exhibits passion and strength with a delicious femininity. I wanted to create a look for Nadiya that projected this same hot-blooded womanliness without overpowering her delicate features. By the time we were through, Nadiya smoldered with a look that could melt any man who crossed her path.

Scott + Nadiya Talk ...

SCOTT: Do you normally wear makeup?

NADIYA: I normally use a little bit of makeup—usually some mascara, some black eyeliner, some lip gloss, a little bit of blush, and sometimes some under-eye concealer.

SCOTT: Do you think there's a difference between American women and Ukrainian women in their approach to beauty?

NADIYA: I think American women are more casual in their approach to beauty, but they display more taste than Russian women, who tend to overdo things.

SCOTT: Do you have a strict skin-care regimen?

NADIYA: Not really—except I use a French skin cream, Embryolisse, that I've been using for years. It's the best. I use it morning and night.

SCOTT: Do you have any beauty secrets?

NADIYA: Well, if I tell you it won't be a secret! I think the most important thing is to keep well hydrated and to exercise regularly.

(continued on page 77)

Creating Nadiya's Look

1

2

3

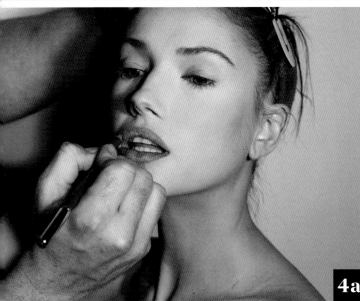

4a

4b

There's something feminine about the cleft in Nadiya's chin and her heart-shaped face. I wanted to give Nadiya a sultry look that would take her to the Isle of Capri. My decision to go in this direction actually had more to do with Nadiya's alluring demeanor than it did with her features.

1 Contouring, concealer, and foundation

Achieving a sultry look for Nadiya depends more on shading and highlighting to really sharpen and refine her delicate features.
(a) Using light strokes with a goat hair brush, I applied contouring (dark) foundation: • Underneath the jaw line • Underneath the cheekbones • Down the sides of the nose • Underneath the tip of the nose • At the inner eye where the bridge of the nose meets the brow bone **(b)** Using a goat hair concealer brush, I applied highlighting (light) concealer using short brush strokes: • Under the eyes • Down the tip of the nose • In the middle of the forehead • At the centre of the chin **(c)** Using a separate goat hair brush, I applied a thin layer of cream pale beige foundation all over her face, which I thoroughly blended with the contouring and highlighting for a smooth finish. *Remember: Effective application of contouring, highlighting, and foundation is about blending, blending, blending. Also, remember to apply some foundation underneath your chin and part way down your neck and blend thoroughly so there's no makeup line between your face and your neck, which is usually lighter than your face.*

2 Cheeks

Moving the blush brush in a circular motion, I blended a very pale flesh-tone peach cream blush on the apples of her cheeks. A darker blush would have looked too heavy with her dark hair.

3 Setting the look

With a very small concealer brush, I applied translucent powder in the following places to create an even, more porcelain-looking finish: • Under the eyes • On the side of the nostrils • On the top of the cheekbones

4 Lips

Nadiya had a nice full bottom lip and a slightly thinner top lip, so balancing out the lips and creating fuller lips overall required liner and lots of high gloss. **(a)** I followed Nadiya's lip line with a brown eyebrow pencil. For this particular look, I wanted a brown colour that didn't have a lot of pink in it, but I also didn't want the harshness of a dark brown. **(b)** I finished her lips with pale pink gloss for a pouty, highly feminine look.

(continued from page 75)

SCOTT: And what do you do to stay in shape?
NADIYA: I like swimming. I like running. It's not that I go to the gym every day, but three or four times a week I try to get to the gym. Maybe I'm doing too much cardio, because I'm not very good at lifting weights. In the summer, I also ride my bike a lot. Now I want to try boxing. I've been into boxing since I was a young girl.

SCOTT: What is it about boxing that you like?
NADIYA: I think everybody thinks boxing is a very harsh sport, but what I like is that it's all about technique. It's a very smart game. It's a very interesting game that is about the way you have to move, from which corner you have to fight your partner. I like the strategy in it.

SCOTT: Is there anything you'd like to change about your look?
NADIYA: That's an interesting question. It really depends on the day. Some days I wake up and I like my face, but other days I wake up and I'm like, "Oh God..." There are many things I do and don't like about my face. It's strange about my face, because a lot of people say that my features are not

(continued on page 79)

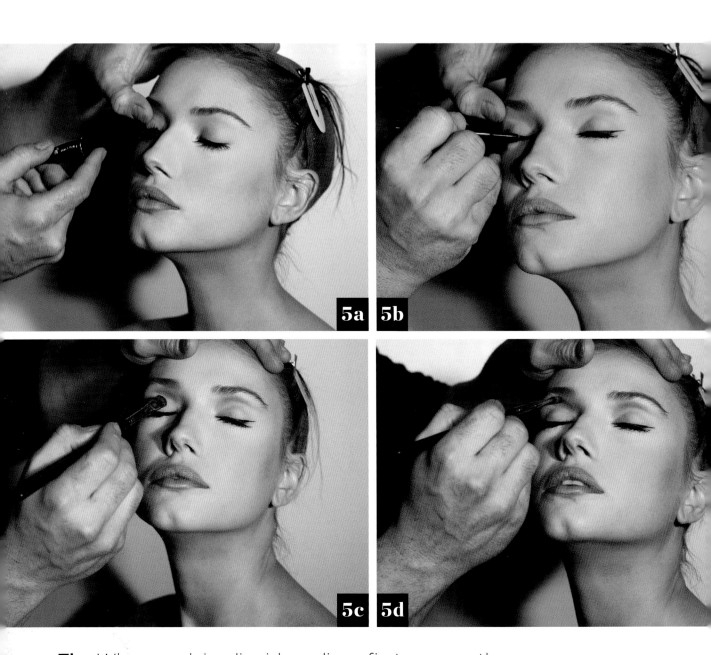

5a   5b

5c   5d

Tip When applying liquid eye liner, first remove the excess liquid on the palm of your hand (not on a tissue where it can pick up fibers). Then, wave the wand around a little so that it's not so wet; this gives you more control when applying the line, without applying excess colour. If you mess up your liquid eyeliner...simply grab a Q-tip, lick it, and wipe away the liner. Saliva is the fastest (and cheapest) makeup corrector on the market!

I followed Nadiya's lip line with a
BROWN EYEBROW PENCIL.

5 Eyes

This look was about creating a very "open eye," so I started with mascara. **(a)** I applied black mascara on the upper and lower lashes. **(b)** I curled Nadiya's lashes after applying the mascara since she told me her lashes were resistant to curling. So the mascara acted as a kind of gel to help hold the curl in place—a good trick for "styling" those hard-to-curl lashes. **(c)** I applied black liquid eyeliner to create a cat-eye effect. I drew a line across the top of her lid and extended the tail past the eye, making sure to keep it on an upward angle. The upward angle helps to lift the outside of the eye, creating a sexy cat-eye effect. I used a liquid eyeliner for Nadiya, instead of a pencil eyeliner, since liquid liners can provide a sharper, bolder effect as opposed to softer, smudgier pencils. **(d)** I applied a Smoky-Tan eye shadow above the normal crease in her eye to create more space on the lid. I used this colour for a smokier, sexier effect on the eyes. Finally, I went back in with a beige eye shadow on the lid and on the brow bone so that it would give the effect of popping out these areas. Remember, light lifts.

Tip When lining your lips, feel free to use what you can find. You can certainly use a lip liner. Sometimes, you might find a colour you like, but the pencil might be labeled as an "eyebrow pencil." You can still use it for lining your lips. In fact, eyebrow pencils have a bit more staying power because they have a denser consistency.

(continued from page 77)

quite perfect. And it's true—when you look at me, you see that one side of my face is a little bit different than the other side of my face. I think the right side is skinnier and the left side is puffier. But I don't want to change anything. I like the way I am. Obviously, I'm not perfect, but I'm doing my best to keep my body in shape and my skin looking good.

SCOTT: Are there other things you're passionate about?
NADIYA: I'm passionate about travelling and living life without worrying too much about whether the things you wish for come to you. Because life is too short, you have to try to be positive and not get too stressed. We have only one life, and we've got to try to do our best. If you really want something in life and you believe very strongly, maybe not today, not tomorrow, but it will happen to you.

SCOTT: Is there something you want strongly for yourself?
NADIYA: Yes, there are so many things. Sometimes I wish for very simple things: having a good family, a nice house with kids and dogs, and to be happy and healthy. But I'd like to go back to

(continued on page 81)

6a

6b

By the time we were through, Nadiya smoldered with a look that **could melt any man** who crossed her path.

(continued from page 79)

6 Completing the look

For the fun of it, I decided to give Nadiya a beauty mark just above her lips. **(a)** Just above her lips I applied a small dot using the black liquid eyeliner. **(b)** I then went back over the dot with the smoky tan eye shadow I used for her eyes to help set the liner and give the beauty mark a more natural look. I used a small pointed brush that is normally used for applying a eyeliner.

Tip When creating a beauty mark, never just put a black spot on your face because it will look like a black spot on your face. This is a two-step process. Go back over it after it dries with a brown eye shadow to cover it. This softens the harshness of the black and doesn't make it look like you have dirt on your face.

school to study political science. I would like to go into politics.

SCOTT: Why politics?
NADIYA: I recently started going to this soup kitchen, the Food Bank in Harlem, New York. I was helping by cooking and serving food for homeless people. It is very hard work, and at the end of the day, you realize you have a good life with family and a good job these people just don't have. It's a very sad scene, even for the people who stand there ten hours a day trying to help these homeless people. These people who work at the Food Bank—the chef and the other people who help prepare and deliver the food—they work so hard. I found it very inspiring and decided that I also want to help people, but in a bigger way. I have traveled and seen much of the world. I see so many people in the world less fortunate than people in the U.S. when it comes to human rights. I would like to help make a difference somehow with all of that. I think we all have a responsibility to help each other.

Nadiya's Reaction
to Her Transformation

"I have never seen any other makeup artist do what Scott does, and I've worked with a lot of makeup artists. So, I was extremely surprised. For example, it's very impressive the way he starts working on your face. He does a mask first and then a face massage. I was most impressed with the way Scott does the skin. It's very interesting the way he applies the base; he has such a different technique. The French are always talking about how

you should start with a good base: the skin. And Scott has a way
of covering up all the imperfections of the skin before starting
to apply the makeup. I now know how to make my skin look like
porcelain when I want this kind of look. Really, Scott showed me
just how far I could go with my makeup to create a different 'me.'
Much further than I ever realized."

Breaking it Down

People approach makeup application with different degrees of experience. The trick is to not be afraid of it. It's only makeup; it washes off. Always feel free to make mistakes.

My aim with this chapter is to provide you with makeup application guidelines and tips based on many years of experience in the industry. It's impossible to cover everything in one chapter, so I'll address those things I feel make the biggest difference for achieving the best possible results.

The finer the brush bristles, the smoother your makeup will go on.

Brushes

Everyone has her preferred method of makeup application. Some people use sponges, some use fingers, and others use cotton balls and Q-tips. I use brushes. I believe brushes offer the ability to move the makeup around the face in a more fluid manner, as well as giving me more control in makeup application, which results in the smoothest blending possible.

I use brushes for every kind of makeup: cream, powder, and liquid. There is a misconception that brushes are best used for powder. But if you're using a brush with high quality bristles, it moves the makeup around just as well as any sponge will. It also effectively blends the makeup into the skin, instead of resting on top of the skin.

I could write a whole book on brushes, since there are so many different kinds. But who wants to read a book about makeup brushes? Instead of covering every kind of brush on the planet, here are some rules of thumb: ● Natural-hair makeup brushes (with bristles made from sable, squirrel, goat, or pony hair) are often much finer and softer and pick up makeup more

easily than most synthetic (nylon or polyester) brushes, which are usually courser and stronger.
● Natural-hair brushes are best used for powders; synthetic brushes are best used for cream or water-based products. ● Brushes need some loving at least once a month. That means washing them thoroughly with soap and water. Baby shampoo works well. This can help extend the life of your brush for years. Also, when drying, be sure to lay your brushes flat so the water doesn't drip down into the ferrule and loosen the glue holding the bristles in place. Loose glue makes for shedding bristles. ● Brushes vary in price, from inexpensive (£4 – £8) to expensive, "professional-grade" (£10 – £25) brushes. Obviously, the more expensive the brush, the higher in quality the materials and craftsmanship will be when it comes to the bristles, the brush handle, and the way the bristles are wrapped for minimal bristle loss over time.

With that in mind, you may be asking, "Are expensive brushes really worth the additional money?"

You bet they are. If you want to achieve the highest-quality look, you've got to care about how you're applying your makeup. Blending and details matter. The finer the brush bristles, the smoother your makeup will go on. Streaky, cakey makeup is not pretty! Also, you'll save yourself time and money in the long run by not having to continually replace cheap brushes.

You can always build your set one brush at a time after you've got your basic brushes, which should consist of the following:
● Tapered contouring brush ● Small concealer brush ● Foundation brush ● Blush brush ● Large powder brush for applying translucent powder

Here are some additional brushes worth investing in: ● Highlighter brush (looks like a fan) for applying shimmer highlight to cheekbones ● Three eye shadow brushes: the largest for applying the base eye colour, a smaller brush for applying colour in the crease, and a thin chiseled brush for applying a line of shadow around the rim of the eye ● Angled brow brush

I could go on and on about different brushes and their uses. I love brushes and so should you. A good brush can take you places, and it's worth spending a little time shopping for them and learning about all the different kinds available. I suggest hitting a makeup counter on a weekday afternoon when business is slow and asking one of those friendly makeup experts to demonstrate all the different brushes. Most of them are usually excited to offer advice and demonstrate various application techniques.

Good brushes, like good makeup, are worth the investment. Remember, you're worth it!

Some More Essentials

Creating your most beautiful self doesn't require a lot of makeup. It's more about good makeup application and having the right equipment. So, before you splurge on the latest eye colours or lipsticks, make sure you've got these essentials:

Airbrush and liquid foundation	No longer just for commercial artists and illustrators, this is a terrific application tool to have in your arsenal. You can apply a very thin layer of liquid foundation. They're worth the money (approx. £100) to achieve an even, feels-like-no-makeup coverage.
Blushes (2)	You should have one cream and one powder blush. Make sure at least one of them is a natural-looking colour (soft rose or peach tones usually work best). The other colour can be something bolder, more dramatic. You can always expand from there.
Brushes (5)	This is my tool of choice for makeup application, as discussed earlier.
Cigarette lighter	Have this on hand for warming your Maybelline eyeliner pencil (more on this later).
Contouring foundation	Contouring with makeup is cheaper than plastic surgery.
Eye drops	An eye solution such as Naphcon-A is great for removing redness from your eyes, as well as for masking red spots such as pimples.
Eye shadows (6 colours)	Brown, black, smoky gray, beige, mustardy yellow, and burgundy are great colours that work on everybody's skin and are best for achieving a more natural look. Like blush, you can always expand your colour palette.
Eye pencils (2)	You should have one black and one brown eye pencil. I use Maybelline pencils. They're classic pencils that can be used in several different ways.
Eyebrow razor and a mini comb	The razor is invaluable for trimming eyebrows and removing facial hair. The mini comb can be any fine-toothed comb sized for use in small areas, such as an eyelash or mustache comb.
False-eyelash adhesive	Without this you would have to staple on your false eyelashes, and that gets messy! The brand I prefer is Duo.

Eyelash curler	Shu Uemura is the best eyelash curler on the planet. It costs a little more—about £19.50—but it's worth every penny. This curler is a bit wider and less curved, so it fits more eye shapes. It works particularly well on Asian eyes.
Facial moisturizer, light	It's always a good idea to moisturize before applying makeup. This helps to soften your skin and get rid of any dry patches.
False eyelashes (2 pair)	This is one of my favourite ways to add drama. They come as individual lashes or in strips. Have fun and experiment!
Foundation	For everyday, be sure to have foundation that matches your natural skin tone. A shade darker or lighter should be used for creating a particular look. Also, don't be afraid to mix two colours of foundation for a better match to your skin. (See "Applying Foundation" below for more on colour selection.)
Highlighting concealer	This is one of the secret ingredients for creating the "glow"
Hydrating mask	This is good for moisturizing prior to makeup application.
Lip liner	A nude or flesh tone, something in line with your natural lip colour, works best for just about everyone.
Luminizing mist	This helps you achieve that glow of young skin.
Mascara	Black is always better than brown; otherwise, what's the point?
Powder puffs	Powder puffs are great for pressing translucent powder into the skin and setting your foundation and blush.
Sheer lip gloss	Use gloss as a quick and easy way to freshen up your look. It's never out of style since moist, shiny lips are always sexy!
Shimmer highlight	For use on cheekbones, splurge on the good stuff. A little bit goes a long way, so it will last you awhile.
Translucent powder	This is good for all skin colours. Translucent literally means "through which light passes."
Tweezers	Tweezers are a necessity for plucking those evil little stragglers.

Lift the eyebrow
with the MINI COMB
and turn in the opposite
direction before trimming.

Preparing the Canvas

Before we get into some basics of makeup application, here are a few things you can do to prepare your face—the canvas—for the best possible results. You don't have to do these things on a daily basis, but the more attention you can give to prepping your face, the more remarkable the final picture will be.

Trimming and Shaping Your Eyebrows

Eyebrows are a prominent feature on the face—as prominent as the nose or lips—so be sure to give them some love.

For starters, make sure they're neat. I'm not an eyebrow fanatic. Some people get crazy about their eyebrows being perfect. I like it when they look more natural as opposed to perfectly manicured. Essentially, you want your eyebrows to lie flat on your face so they look smooth.

In addition to smoothing them down, you can also experiment with different shapes. But you want to be careful about how you do this. I recommend using a razor comb instead of tweezers for trimming and shaping. You can find razor combs everywhere, and they're cheap! To use a razor comb, follow these steps: **(1)** Put the mini comb in the hairs of the eyebrow **(2)** Turn the mini comb in the opposite direction to LIFT the brow hairs off the face. **(3)** Trim with razor. **(4)** Check the eyebrow by smoothing the hairs before trimming some more.

Remember to lift and trim the brow hairs little by little and check in between each trim to avoid cutting the brows too short.

Apply a tiny dab of gel or hair wax to help smooth down the brows after trimming.

The things I love about using a razor comb as opposed to plucking with tweezers are that you don't get ingrown hairs and if you decide you want to grow your brows back, you haven't taken out the follicle, which is what you do when you pluck. Once the follicle is removed, it takes much longer for the brow to grow back. Eyebrow styles change all the time, so give yourself the option of growing out your eyebrows and changing their shape. Remember the women from the 1950s? They plucked so much they couldn't grow their eyebrows back. I always say pluck as little as possible.

Many women end up with what I call "sperm brow" that clips up and then back around and looks like a little sperm whale. This has the effect of closing in your eye on the inside corner, because the brow nearest your nose is too heavy. Not a pretty look! The idea is to shape your eyebrows so that you lift and open up the eyes. You can experiment with many different shapes to find what kind of look you prefer, especially if you're trimming and not tweezing.

Neat Trick

Shaping Eyebrows with Wax

You can mold your eyebrows with wax instead of plucking with tweezers or trimming with a razor comb. I use Geisha wax. Since your eyebrows naturally grow down from the top and up from the bottom of the brow, you can make them narrower by pulling them up with wax. It's good to do this when you're in the transitional phase of trying to grow out your brows for a new shape.

Tip If you have red hair and you want to match your eyebrow colour with your hair colour, don't apply red or brown colour to your brow, which usually tends to look too dark. Instead, add yellow to the brow, because that's all red hair is: a lot of gold in brown hair. Using yellow achieves a golden red eyebrow, which will look more natural than a brown eyebrow.

Addressing Facial Hair

The other thing you want to consider is the amount of facial hair you have on your face apart from your eyebrows. Whether we like it or not, our society has come to value clean, smooth skin on women. Men can usually get away with just about any kind of facial hair. But that's probably because they have other things to worry about, like receding hairlines. So, take a good look at yourself and see whether you have a significant amount of hair on your upper lip or on the sides of your face. If you have a mustache or sideburns or excessive fuzz on any part of your face, you should remove it in whatever way you feel most comfortable. I recommend using a razor comb, because it's a quick, cheap, easy way to groom.

Many Mediterranean and Middle Eastern women (e.g., Italian, Greek, and Persian) tend to have more hair on the sides of their face and upper lip. Many of them use electrolysis to get rid of the fuzz. But if you don't have money for electrolysis, I recommend just using a razor, because the hair doesn't grow back any thicker. (The idea that hair grows back thicker after shaving is an old wives' tale.) Also, a razor doesn't pull and stretch the skin like waxing does.

The goal is to keep your face as hair-free as possible so you have a smooth, porcelain-like surface on which to apply your makeup.

Electrolysis can be very costly and very painful, but it's a permanent solution, as is laser hair removal. For laser removal to work, you have to have fair skin and dark hair; otherwise, the laser will burn you and you'll walk out with blisters since the laser doesn't register the hair as well and takes longer to zap the follicle.

If waxing is the route you choose to go, make sure you go to a good waxer, preferably someone who is recommended to you. Problems such as stretched skin, wax burn, or a skin rash can result if you use someone who isn't an expert waxer. So, don't be afraid to ask your friends for a referral. A bad waxer can do more damage, and it's just not worth the risk.

Removing Redness in the Skin

If you're dealing with a pimple or a breakout, apply a couple of eye drops to the irritated spot. This will reduce the redness a little, which makes the spot easier to cover with makeup. But it's not an acne killer. It simply constricts the blood vessels as it would in your eyes. Remember, this is a temporary fix. Be sure to speak to your dermatologist if you're experiencing red, blotchy skin or rosacea on a regular basis.

Also, yellow works wonders to combat redness. So, a foundation with a bit more of a peachy, yellowish tone works well for countering red skin.

Hydrating the Face

I often begin any makeover by applying a hydrating mask for ten minutes. It moisturizes the face, softens the eyes, and reduces any inflammation in the skin. If you don't have time for a mask, you can simply apply some light moisturizer and then wait a couple of minutes for the skin to absorb it before applying your makeup. Light moisturizing is an important step since it balances your skin for more even makeup application. Feel free to hydrate as often as once a week.

Relaxing the Face:
The Lymphatic Drain

I learned this little trick in Shiatsu school. Your scalp and face are connected right at the ears and the jaw. If you press on the ears and the jaw, it hurts like hell, but it relaxes all the muscles in your face. When you sleep, you clench your jaw; when you drive you tense your facial muscles from the stress. You want to get rid of that tension by relaxing the muscles in your face with a lymphatic drain. The best part is, you can do this yourself.

I do this with all my clients before red carpet events and photography sessions. It's especially effective after you've been flying. On a plane, the air is stale and you can't move around, so the blood doesn't circulate well throughout your body. A lymphatic drain helps drain the sinuses and gets your circulation going, which helps to oxygenate your skin. The results are amazing. A 40-year-old woman can have this process done and it will make her feel like she's thirty-five years old, just by pressing on both sides of her jaw! Now that's a trick worth learning, yes?

Taking a Moment

Once you're groomed, moisturized, and relaxed, you're well on your way to creating your most beautiful self.

But don't do anything just yet. Before applying any makeup, take a moment to appreciate the "you" without makeup. Notice your eye colour, the shape of your lips, your nose, and each and every wrinkle. And as you study your face, fall in love with your features by reminding yourself that they are uniquely yours. Nobody else has the exact same arrangement of features, bone structure, or skin type as you have. Take a few deep breaths. Inhale the beauty of "self." Try to stay focused on the beauty of your individuality, not on your imperfections.

Also, take this time to get a cool, refreshing glass of water. As a general rule, most of us don't drink enough water, so try to get in the habit of using your makeup time as a time to hydrate your body and moisturize from within.

Once you've taken a couple of minutes to give yourself some love, you're ready to begin applying makeup.

Makeup Application

Step into the Light

Lighting is very important when putting on makeup. Be sure to apply your makeup in a well-lit area. That means making sure you have light on both sides of your face. Applying your makeup in front of a window for more natural light is a good idea, only if you aren't being hit by direct sunlight. The reason for this is that in direct sunlight, you tend to put on more makeup to compensate for the intensity of the light. Sunlight is wicked intense light—the most powerful light we have, in fact—and it simply can't be replicated with florescent lighting or 100-watt bulbs. So, you run the risk of looking like a crazy lady with too much makeup. Softer, natural light, similar to a slightly overcast day, is the ideal natural light by which to apply makeup. If possible, check your makeup in a couple of different mirrors with different lighting before walking out the door.

My favourite lighting for makeup application is a halogen bulb. I recommend picking up two cheap halogen lamps for your bathroom or vanity table. Just make sure the light doesn't come from below your chin, since that creates weird monster lighting and you'll end up looking like Boris Karloff. The light should be at the same height as your eye line for the best results.

Blend, Blend, Blend

I can't overemphasize the importance of blending. You'll see the word throughout this book, because it makes all the difference in good makeup application.

The point of blending is to make sure your makeup isn't sitting on top of your skin. You want the makeup to blend in with the natural fluids in your skin.

Want a smooth, flawless finish? Blend, blend, blend!

The best blending is achieved by moving your brush in a soft, circular motion, which helps to avoid lines on your face.

Creating a Smooth Canvas

APPLYING CONCEALER AND CONTOURING

You want to "build the face" by applying concealer and contouring. This is always the first step in the process before applying colour makeup. But it's not about just flattening everything. It's about creating dimension, which is why you contour as well as conceal. Think of it as creating your canvas, which is all about defining your facial bones. Even if your bones are not prominent, you can use contouring and concealer to draw them out more by creating greater contrast in your face.

The rule of thumb for contouring and concealer is as follows: *Light adds to and dark takes away.*

Ultimately, you want to bring light to the centre of your face. This kind of "glow" helps draw focus to the darker, more colourful features on your face—the eyes, brows, and mouth.

SELECTING YOUR CONTOURING AND HIGHLIGHTING COLOURS

The general rule of thumb for selecting foundation for contouring and highlighting is as follows: go one to two shades darker than your normal skin tone for your contouring makeup and one to two shades lighter for highlighting makeup.

It's hard to get any more specific than this because it all depends on the amount of contouring and highlighting you want to do and how dramatic you want the effect to be. You'll see me vary the amount of highlighting and contouring on each woman, depending upon what I felt necessary for their particular look.

Also, I oftentimes use a light cream concealer as a way of creating the highlights when "building the face" in the beginning. Cream concealer has a slightly heavier consistency than that of powder or liquid foundation, which means it has the added advantage of providing more coverage. So, it depends on the amount of coverage you desire as to whether you decide to work with powder-, liquid-, or cream-based makeup for your contouring and highlighting.

APPLYING FOUNDATION

I prefer cream foundation over liquid foundation because cream-based makeup has more mobility—I can move it around more easily and with more control. Ultimately, you should use a foundation that you feel most comfortable with and that you feel works best with your skin. As a general rule, the consistency of cream foundations are good to use if you want more coverage; liquid and powder foundations tend to provide lighter coverage.

When applying your foundation, use a small amount and move your brush in a circular motion, blending all the while. If you're using a cream foundation, simply dip the brush directly into the makeup vial. If you're using a liquid or powder foundation, pour a small amount of foundation in the palm of your hand and dip the brush from there. *Remember, always wash your hands before applying makeup.*

Also, the neck and the face should know each other. So, be sure to take your foundation all the way down your neck. Why stop at the face when you can do your whole body! (Okay, maybe not your WHOLE body...but at least further down to make sure you include the neck.)

Again, the most important thing to remember about applying contouring, concealer, and foundation is that you don't want people to see it when you leave the house. Blend!

Selecting your foundation colour

There are many different options when choosing your foundation colour, so it can be a little overwhelming. But choosing the right colour is easier than you think: simply match your foundation colour to the colour of skin on your collar bone or chest, not on your neck. Your neck is lighter skin than your everyday colouring because it is constantly protected from sunlight by your chin.

APPLYING BLUSH

Cream blush is always better if you have combination skin or you have dry patches on your face because the colour in a cream blush will adhere more consistently across the apples of your cheeks, even if the skin texture isn't consistent. Powder blush, on the other hand, is better for more even-toned, normal skin. On oilier skin or combination skin, powder blush will adhere where the oily spots are and will collect around the dry areas of your face; as a result, you'll wind up with very uneven, blotchy cheeks that don't look smooth. And that's not sexy.

I often see women use blush for contouring underneath the cheeks, instead of using blush to add a touch of colour to the cheeks. I say that if you want to contour and create cheekbones, use contour foundation! Otherwise, you look like you're from the 1980s when you put blush underneath the cheekbone.

When you get flush, you're blushing from underneath. You want to mimic this natural blush when putting on your makeup. So, blend your blush onto the apples of your cheeks and up toward your temple a bit. This is particularly important for women over forty-five. If you apply your blush under your cheekbones, it's just going to draw your face down, and you'll come out looking too gaunt. The idea is to add youth, not age, to your face. And the easiest way to find the apples of your cheeks? Just smile!

ADDING SHIMMER HIGHLIGHTS

Whether or not you have prominent cheekbones, I still recommend highlighting them. The light will help draw the eye to this area and has the effect of "lifting" the face. In the transformations, you can see where I tend to consistently add highlights. Another good way think of it is to touch those "high" spots on your face where light first hits: the nose, the cheekbones, and the forehead.

ACHIEVING A BRONZY LOOK

Everyone feels better with a bit of color. If you are going after the sun-kissed look, start with a very light amount of bronzing powder on your brush and blend in a circular motion for the most natural-looking, warm glow. Build up your bronze slowly by layering. You can always add more, which is easier than trying to remove it. Look to Jessica Murphy's transformation into a bronze goddess for more tips on how to achieve the best fake tan!

Setting Your Makeup

Setting your makeup with translucent powder is an important step in the process that bears emphasis here. If you're going to go to all the work of applying foundation and blush, why would you want it to smear or look greasy? You can also put translucent powder on the eyelids and in the T-zone, before adding eye colour, if you want to create "light" in those areas by mimicking the natural, lighter skin tone of those areas on the face.

Tips on Emphasizing Your Individual Features

The point to remember with makeup application is that you don't want to try to emphasize all features at once. Instead, pick one feature you would like to highlight, and then go for it. If you're stuck in the same old way of doing things—if you normally emphasize your eyes, for instance—change it up a little and go for more dramatic lipstick and less eye makeup. You might be surprised how such a simple shift from one feature to another can dramatically change your look.

Lips

Women sometimes think they can get away wearing nothing on their lips, particularly during the day when going for a more natural look. But it's still important to wear something on your lips, even if it's only a clear gloss or lip balm, to help keep the lips moisturized and protected. Otherwise, you'll find yourself licking your lips a lot, which actually results in dry, cracked lips. Not sexy! Lipstick also helps a woman look more "put together," and even "kissable." And what woman doesn't want that?

LINING THE LIPS

Lining your lips is a useful trick for balancing out the lips (e.g. if your upper lip is thinner than the bottom lip) or if you want to make the lips appear fuller than they really are.

When lining the lips, the idea is not to create a hard line, but rather to provide some definition for the mouth. So, it's better to go with a light touch when lining to provide a more natural look.

Always be sure to line directly on the lip border or just inside it, but never outside the lips; otherwise, you will look like that crazy lady at the mall. And make sure after applying that you softly blend the liner, so you avoid ring-around-the-mouth.

It's important to use a nude or flesh tone lip liner when going for a more natural look. For other colours, it's best to either match your lip liner to your lipstick colour or go only one shade darker than your lipstick colour, as a general rule of thumb.

Creating Fuller Lips

To create fuller lips, draw straight across the peak on your upper lip, without emphasizing the dip in the centre. This creates the illusion that your lips are fuller with that come-to-me pouty look. That's very sexy, no? Be sure when drawing the line across, you don't go higher than the two peaks with the line; otherwise, it will look as if you lined above your natural lip line.

REMOVING DRY SKIN FROM DRY LIPS

Everyone gets dry lips now and again. Luckily, it's easy to remove dry skin from your lips without causing irritation. Apply some lip balm to a mini makeup brush and gently scrub the brush back and forth on your lips to slough off the dead skin. In addition to getting rid of dry skin, you're also providing circulation to the lips, so the lips will appear plumper and with added colour.

If you brush a little bit around the outside of the lips—gently—you can also get rid of any little blackheads that you might have from lip balm, lipstick, and so on.

You can use a toothbrush for this, but I recommend you buy a mini makeup brush with boar's hair bristles instead. These types of bristles have a little better give to them, so you're not destroying your lips.

Eyes

It's well known that "the eyes are the windows to the soul." We communicate so much of who we are and how we feel through our eyes. The eyes are the first feature we go to when greeting someone or when we want to know how the other person feels. Eyes are uniquely our own—no two pair are alike—and as you can see in these transformations, I believe eyes deserve special emphasis.

As you go through the book, you'll notice that I use certain colours to help bring out a particular model's distinct eye colour. My recommendation is to play around with different colour combinations to see which ones compliment your eyes best, using these transformations as a guideline. The trick is to draw out your own eye colour as opposed to overshadowing your eyes (quite literally) with too much coloured makeup. That usually means picking eye shadow colours that contrast with your eye colour, instead of trying to match the colour of your eyes. (Of course, there are exceptions to this general rule too, depending on what look you're trying to achieve.)

These are some additional techniques you might find helpful when addressing certain types of challenges with your eyes:

EYES THAT ARE HOODED

Look in the mirror and stare straight ahead. If you see no eyelid on your eyes, you have hooded eyes. When applying eye shadow in this case, the last thing you want to do is put a light colour on top of this kind of lid because that will make your eyes look puffier and more hooded. So, it's better to go with very minimal eye colour and accentuate the eyes with mascara or fake eyelashes. Lauren Bedford's transformation is a good demonstration of this approach.

EYES THAT ARE TOO FAR APART

If you feel your eyes are too far apart, you can make them appear closer together by drawing the emphasis toward your inner eye. To do this, apply the heaviest portion of mascara or false lashes on the inside corner of your eyes to give the illusion that the eyes are closer together.

CLOSE-SET EYES

If you feel that your eyes are too close together, you can make them appear farther apart by drawing the emphasis toward your outer eye. To do that, apply the heaviest portion of mascara or false lashes on the outside corner to draw the eyes outward.

SMALL OR DEEP-SET EYES

If you have small eyes, put some white cream eye shadow on the inner corner of your eyelids to help open up your eyes. This technique is especially beneficial if you've got deep-set eyes. Oona Hart's transformation is a good example of how to make small eyes appear larger.

Effective Eye Lining with a Pencil

You can flatten out your eyeliner pencil and create an edge to it that allows you to go right up against the lid. I usually drop the pencil straight on the table. It's easier than using an eyeliner with a point, since it allows for a better angle on the pencil.

USING LIQUID EYELINER

Eyeliner has been used for decades to create a dramatic, glamourous effect. Proper application of liquid eyeliner is about removing excess liquid from the wand before applying.

Take the tip of the eyeliner and remove some of the liquid by drawing a couple of lines on the back of your hand. Then wave the eyeliner in the air to help it dry slightly before drawing on your eyelid.

Keep in mind that heavy eyeliner has the effect of closing up the eye. So, I don't necessarily recommend it if you're using false eyelashes. The whole point of the lashes is to create open, fluttery, flirty eyes. So, think twice before lining the eye as well.

If you do decide to use eyeliner with false eyelashes, be sure to draw all the way to the inner corner of the top eyelid with the liner so that the line doesn't stop short where the eyelashes stop.

Tip Sometimes leaving the eyes alone works best. In other words, let the colour of your concealer come through on the eyelid instead of putting on eye shadow. You can always add some false eyelashes to accentuate your eyes, instead of covering your eyes in a lot of heavy colour. Sometimes less is more.

Working with a Maybelline Eye Pencil

A Maybelline eye pencil is my black pencil of choice. It is the blackest pencil I know. It's the least expensive pencil on the market and it can work both as an eyeliner and as an eyebrow pencil. But before you use it for lining your eyes, you first want to soften it; otherwise, it pulls on the skin due to its harder consistency and creates wrinkles, and who needs those? All you need is a cigarette lighter. Simply wave the tip of the pencil through the flame a couple of times to soften it.

Remember to blow on it and test it on your hand before putting it on your eye!

The consistency should be firm, to the point that it glides. It should not be wet, and you shouldn't be able to bend the tip. (If it goes on too soft, it will clump up in your eye and irritate it.) Once it cools down almost to the point of getting hard again, you can use it like a crayon, and the effect will be like a soft charcoal pencil.

APPLYING MASCARA

For really lush lashes, I recommend colouring both the underneath and the top of the lashes. To avoid clumpy lashes, lay the mascara brush at the base of the lashes, jiggle the brush from side to side, and then whisk it up through the rest of the lashes. This loads the mascara at the base of the lashes. It doesn't leave you with clumpy ends but still looks really thick and luscious.

As far as colour goes, I use black mascara—always. What's the point of using anything but black? That's like saying, "Hi, I'm going to pretend like I'm putting mascara on, but I'm really not!" If you want people to see your eyes, black is the only way to go.

USING FALSE EYELASHES

I love false eyelashes. They're a great way to make your eyes look bigger and add drama. Just make sure you don't wait until an hour before your big event to learn how to apply them. It takes a little practice and patience to learn how to apply them so that they look natural.

When you use false eyelashes correctly, they never look "costumey." You can go heavy on the lash with a gown or a beautiful dress or a trench coat. If you use a heavier lash, just be sure not to overdo it by also applying a lot of eye shadow. Less is more in this case because you're picking one feature and you're taking it all the way there, which makes a bolder statement. It's better than adding a colour on every part of the face. I get really tired of colour, which is odd for a makeup artist to say.

Proper application

Make sure your lashes are clean before applying faux lashes, which adhere to both your eyelid and your natural eyelashes. It's a good idea to put the eyelashes up to your eye to see how long they are before adding adhesive. Sometimes you may need to trim the false eyelashes, if they look unnaturally long—unless, of course, you prefer to look like a drag queen.

Apply the adhesive to the strip of eyelashes (not to your eyelid) and set the lashes along your natural lash line. You have a few seconds to adjust the lashes as the glue begins to dry.

There are two types of eyelash adhesive: temporary and semi-permanent. Temporary lasts until you apply water to the adhesive. Semi-permanent can last up to five days.

Sometimes you might decide that demi lashes (half lashes) are all you need for opening up the eye, instead of a whole strip. You can cut the eyelash in half and apply either one or both halves to the outside or inside corner of your eye, depending on the look you want to create.

Proper removal

Use an oil-based remover to remove false eyelashes. Never pull the eyelashes off without using a remover; otherwise, you risk pulling and stretching your delicate eyelid skin. Treat your eyes with care!

Applying individual lashes

Individual lashes give you much more control over the look and feel of the lash. I often use individual lashes when I want to give a more open, airy feeling to the eye. Placement of individual lashes is key. Applying the lashes to the outside corner keeps the eye more open. Applying the lashes to the inside corner creates a more doe-eyed effect. Or you can apply them in different directions for a star-burst effect. Adhering individual lashes can be a little tricky at first, but they provide many more options once you get the hang of them.

Hands and Nails

Hands are a very feminine feature on a woman. Or at least they can be if they are well manicured. There's nothing tackier than a beautiful woman with dry hands and unkempt nails. Beautiful hands can actually turn a person on, so don't forget this important step when beautifying.

I always like it when the nails look clean and look like an extension of your hand. It's sexy. I don't like seeing really bright colours on long nails. I think too much red and pink on white skin pulls out the red in the skin. This emphasizes the redness on the knuckles and in the cuticles because red fingernails make whatever's red in your skin look even redder. If your nails are dressed with a more natural colour, it makes for a better blend from hand to nail, and it elongates the fingers (So, this is a good point to remember if you've got short, stubby fingers!). A light beige polish looks great. A French manicure is always good.

There are some exceptions to the rule of natural colour on long nails, though: ● **Women of colour:** Women with really dark skin tones can pull off brighter colours without a problem. ● **Shorter nails:** If you want to sport shorter nails, some of the darker colours—burgundy, chocolate, black, navy—can be fun. So knock yourself out.

When in doubt, go without a colour. But still moisturize your hands and make sure the nails are smooth and trimmed. Not only do beautiful hands look more feminine, they make you feel more feminine!

Of course, the same goes for feet. Don't subject everybody to rough heels and fungus toes. Get in the habit of treating your feet to a pedicure—either in home or at a salon—at least once a month to help address these issues. In the case of polish on toenails, go for colour. Hot pink or red toenails are oh, so sexy!

Transformations

Oona:
Bringing Sensuality to the Forefront by Playing Up the Eyes

Oona is one smart cookie who isn't easily impressed. She lets her guard down slowly—not because she's apprehensive but because she doesn't need anybody telling her how to do things. She stays attuned to current events, and she has her opinions. Although Oona models, her world is not about her appearance. It's about her family—she's married with a two-year-old son—and her two passions: photography and painting.

Oona has warm, intelligent eyes that seemed to flirt with me when she spoke. Unfortunately, they were dwarfed by her more prominent cheekbones and mouth. I knew that once we shifted the focus to her enticing eyes, Oona's sensuality would come hurtling to the forefront. In the end, not only did Oona lose her cool demeanor, she became undeniably hot.

SCOTT: What is your typical morning beauty regimen?
OONA: I don't have a routine. I'm not really rigid about that sort of thing. Sometimes when I get up in the morning, I do nothing. If I'm going to work, I will wash my face and put moisturizer on. I wash my face before bed. Sometimes I use something cute and fancy and sometimes it's just a bar of soap in the shower. I use a heavy moisturizer at night usually, but not always.

SCOTT: Today you didn't come with much makeup on. Is that because you don't prefer to wear makeup?
OONA: I love makeup. I'm not somebody that wears it all the time—I don't feel naked without it—but I enjoy wearing it, like when I'm doing something festive. I think when I was younger I experimented more with makeup, but now I don't have the time as much as I used to because my son will come over and grab some eye shadow and run into the other room.

(continued on page 111)

Creating Oona's Look

Tip When bronzing, make sure you leave the centre of the face alone so that you don't darken it. Think of it as creating a diamond shape of light at the centre of your face.

Oona exuded a sex appeal even when she was trying to downplay her beauty by wearing no makeup, beat-up jeans, boots, and a tank top. She has a combination of vulnerability, toughness, and sensuality, all the necessary ingredients for an explosion. Bombshell!

---

1 Contouring, highlighting, and foundation

Oona clearly has a prominent bone structure, so the contouring for her was minimal, more like adding a blush than creating a hollow. **(a)** Using a goat hair brush, I applied minimal contouring (dark) foundation: • Underneath the jaw line (slight contour) • Underneath the cheekbones • On the sides of the nose • At the temples • Under the tip of the nose (gives the illusion of shortening the nose) **(b)** Using a concealer brush, I applied highlighting (light) concealer: • On top of the cheekbones • Underneath the eyebrows • Under the eyes • On the bridge of the nose • At the centre of the chin **(c)** Using a separate goat hair brush, I applied a thin layer of a very neutral beige foundation on top of the contouring and highlighting. *Remember: Blend thoroughly, moving the brush in a circular motion to marry all the colours together for a seamless transition.*

2 Setting the look

I finished off with a nice dusting of translucent powder for setting the makeup and providing a seamless finish. Using a small powder brush, I applied translucent powder: • On top of the cheekbones • Underneath the eyebrows • On the bridge of the nose • At the centre of the chin

3 Bronzing

Using a large powder brush, I applied a pale bronzing powder, moving upward from the neck and jaw line to her cheeks and working the brush in a circular motion. This creates a very soft effect in the cheek area.

(continued from page 109)

SCOTT: Do you have any features you like or dislike?

OONA: I don't know if I have a specific feature, at least not one that you use makeup on! Sometimes I wake up and feel really good about the way I look, and other days I feel a little busted. But I think that's the same for everybody. No matter how glamourous I might look to somebody else, I have those days when I wake up and I feel great and those days I don't. But I don't really think about how I look every day, and if I did, I might be less satisfied. Maybe that's the trick: You just can't think about it too much, just an appropriate amount to have some self-respect. But not so much that you become too critical because anybody can overdo the self-criticism, which just doesn't do anybody any good.

SCOTT: How does a person avoid being overly critical of herself?

OONA: I think you have to like your life, and then a lot of things become beautiful.

SCOTT: What do you like to do for fun?

OONA: I have a kid, so I play with him. And I have a man, so I play with him too. My kid is two.

(continued on page 113)

4 Cheeks

This look requires only a bronzing powder as a blush. So, I applied no blush whatsoever on Oona's cheeks.

5 Lips

I used a transparent shimmer gloss to accentuate Oona's mouth. Oona has very full lips, so no lip lining was necessary.

6 Eyes

To demonstrate the subtlety of the eye shadow, I finished one eye to show the effect it has on opening the eye. This is how it broke down: **(a)** I had Oona curl her own lashes. **(b)** I used just a splash of the bronzer for minimal covering on the whole lid. You want a light touch here to avoid putting on too much colour and giving a heavy, over-tanned look. **(c)** I applied a basic chocolate-brown shadow from the lash line of the upper lid to just about above the crease. **(d)** I surrounded the rest of the eye with this same chocolate-brown shadow to create a lot of depth with a neutral tone. **(e)** I topped off the eye with individual false eyelashes on the upper and lower eyelids. I used individual lashes because I wanted the lashes to feel very fluffy, which you can't always achieve with a strip of false eyelashes. **(f)** The last thing I did was apply white eyeliner on the inside of her lower eyelid to help open up the eye. This gives the effect of creating a larger eyeball.

7 Eyebrows

I liked the shape of Oona's eyebrows, but they were just a bit furry for the furry lashes. So for minimal shaping, I opted to use stiff hair wax and a bit of hairspray. Here's what I did: **(a)** I applied the eyebrow wax on the brow with my fingers, sweeping upward. **(b)** With a credit card, I pushed the eyebrow down and pinched the hairs together, creating a thinner brow without plucking.

Voilà! Thinner eyebrows!

Tip You can warm up your eyelash curler by rubbing the part you apply to the lashes back and forth between your fingers so that it works more like a curling iron.

(continued from page 111)

He tests his boundaries, but he's far from terrible. He's really amazing. Otherwise, I spend my time either painting or doing photography.

SCOTT: Where did the photography interests come from?
OONA: My dad's a photographer, and I grew up assisting him in the studio. I've been doing photography as long as I can remember. I photograph in the old-fashioned way because I learned those techniques from my dad. So, I prefer shooting with film and large-format cameras.

SCOTT: Are you strict with yourself when it comes to food and drink?
OONA: I don't eat meat. That's probably my only thing that's an absolute. I'm not a vegetarian. I eat fish, but I don't eat meat. And I eat fish because if I don't eat any meat, I can't really go anywhere exotic. By allowing myself to eat fish, I can usually get by.

SCOTT: What do you think it takes to be beautiful?
OONA: I think it's important to be happy. I think if you're happy, you can be happy with yourself, you can find other things encouraging and beautiful and positive, and you can be beautiful yourself.

REACTIONS...

Oona's Reaction to Her Transformation

"It was a huge transformation. I looked fantastic. No one had ever made me up exactly as Scott did. Every time you're made up, it's different, but I've never seen myself quite the same way before. My eyes were definitely more prominent. And I learned some great techniques. I've incorporated his eyebrow trick into my regular routine."

Elizabeth:
Using Airbrush Foundation for Added Radiance and Distinction

Elizabeth stopped teaching years ago, yet she's anything but retired. She continues to work as a substitute teacher, volunteers as a horseback riding instructor on weekends, stays actively involved in the lives of her three daughters, and spends as much time as possible with her five-year-old grandson. Oh, she also "does some movie and commercial work on the side." Elizabeth is a pro-age woman who believes in taking good care of herself and keeping up her appearance. Elizabeth has a naturally handsome countenance, and I was excited about enhancing her strong Irish features, particularly her sparkling emerald-green eyes. In the end, a more distinguished Elizabeth emerged with a new look that spans from city chic to equestrian elegance.

Scott + Elizabeth Talk ...

SCOTT: What's important to you in life?

ELIZABETH: My family—I have three daughters and a grandson, and I try to spend as much time with him as possible. We went ice skating recently—he loved that. And of course, we have fun in the park. We do whatever sounds like fun together.

SCOTT: Would you mind telling me your age?

ELIZABETH: I'd rather respond with the old cliché, "Age is just a number." It's how you feel, how you act, and how you think about things; that's what's important. I don't feel old, so why should I be saddled with a specific number so that people who don't know me will automatically dismiss me as being old and with outdated ideas? I know people who are old at forty, and I know others who are young at eighty. It's all in the mindset.

SCOTT: As a beautiful woman, how do you feel about getting older?

ELIZABETH: Let's face it: Ageing is inevitable.

(continued on page 119)

Creating Elizabeth's Look

1a

1b

1c

2

Tip When using an airbrush to apply foundation, it's very important to cover your hair, particularly if you're fair-haired. A bandana, a stocking cap, or even a hair band works—just something to pull the hair off your face and protect your hair from being covered in a mist of makeup!

Elizabeth is a beautiful woman with a strong chin, nose, and eyes. She also has ruddy skin, which is not surprising since skin tone usually changes as we age. By emphasizing her strong points, I felt we could modernize Elizabeth's look to give her a more distinguished appearance.

1 Contouring, highlighting, and foundation

This was a very simple process with Elizabeth. I opted to use an airbrush to apply Elizabeth's foundation. Airbrushing has the effect of looking and feeling like there is virtually no makeup on the face. Heavier foundations on mature skin can sometimes make a person appear older, since the makeup often settles in the creases of the skin. I wanted to provide just enough foundation on Elizabeth to eliminate the redness in her skin but still even out her skin tone.

I had to put a stocking cap on Elizabeth's head, much to her chagrin. This ultimately prevented her extremely light hair from turning brown as a result of the makeup. **(a)** Using a concealer brush, I applied a very small amount of highlighting (light) concealer just to add some light: ● Underneath the eyes **(b)** Using an airbrush, I applied a pinky-beige foundation all over her face and neck.

2 Lips

Elizabeth called her lips "less than voluptuous." This is not surprising, since our lips naturally lose collagen and colour as we age. Now listen up, ladies. Don't try to compensate for thinner lips by applying a darker coloured lipstick to make your lips stand out. Applying dark lipstick actually has the effect of making your lips look smaller and creates what I like to call "zipper lips"—lips that look more like a zipper than they do lips. You don't want zipper lips. *Remember: Light adds and dark diminishes. If you want to enhance something, make it lighter. If you want to minimize something, make it darker.* **(a)** I applied a fleshy-beige lip liner with some pink in it to Elizabeth's lips. I wanted a little colour to avoid having a completely nude lip; otherwise, Elizabeth's mouth would disappear completely. **(b)** I finished off with a pale pink lip gloss similar in colour to the lip liner. The softness of the lip gloss creates a softer mouth as opposed to using lipstick, which tends to cake more easily.

(continued from page 117)

My mother used to say, "Just grow old gracefully." What she meant is that we should accept it and not fight it. I think differently. I don't mind getting older, but I don't want to look it, feel it, or act it. I take really good care of my skin, eat healthy food, and exercise. I keep myself active, both in body and in mind. I stay open to new ideas and keep current with the trends. Getting older has given me a kind of freedom. I am much more comfortable in my skin.

SCOTT: Do you think our society regards older women as beautiful, or are we a youth-obsessed society?
ELIZABETH: Yes, I think that some people think older women are beautiful. Meryl Streep, Katherine Hepburn, Sophia Loren—they exude a timeless beauty and have always presented themselves in a positive, confident, and classy way. Unfortunately, I also think we are a youth-obsessed society, which is sad because some of the youthful beauties that are emulated do not have the substance to be role models for today's youth.

SCOTT: How would your daughters describe you?

(continued on page 121)

Tip Remember, your face and neck should know each other. So blend your foundation down past your jawline or else you'll end up with the dreaded makeup line between the face and the neck.

3a

3b

3c

Tip Heavy eyelashes on a mature woman make her look like an ageing theatre star. So, use lighter lashes, unless, of course, you're going for really high drama!

3 Eyes

With Elizabeth, I didn't want to create any kind of "look" where she would appear heavily made up, so I went with subtler shading. **(a)** I applied a subtle eye shadow called Cashmere (a pale brown-gray) in her crease to create hollows in the eye. **(b)** I applied white eyeliner on the inside of her lower eyelid instead of black eyeliner to help open up her eye. Black eyeliner would look too heavy with Elizabeth's fair colouring. **(c)** I added false eyelashes to give her eyes more oomph, but I used a strip in which the lashes were sparse and open. **(d)** I finished off the eyes with lots of black mascara on both the upper and lower lashes.

5 Blush

Elizabeth has terrific cheekbones, so I applied a soft peach cream blush, blending in a circular motion and making sure to stay on the apples of her cheeks. I wanted to use a subtle tone so that her face wouldn't scream, "Hey, I'm wearing blush!" With blush, when in doubt always go subtler; otherwise, you risk looking like Baby Jane Hudson or like you applied your makeup in the dark.

6 Setting the look

I finished off with a nice dusting of translucent powder so as not to change the colour of the foundation and the blush.

4 Eyebrows

Elizabeth doesn't have eyebrows due to years of over-plucking, so I created Elizabeth's eyebrows using an eyebrow pencil. Because of her lighter colouring, I didn't want to go too heavy on her brow. I used a very pale brown eyebrow pencil (almost a camel colour) and followed her brow bone. This colour provides a much warmer look than an icy gray pencil.

Remember: Always opt to use a razor comb for shaping your brows instead of plucking the hairs away. Plucking damages the follicles and eventually the follicles die. Your eyebrows require a bit more maintenance with a razor, but they still look nicely manicured without suffering permanent damage.

Tip Applying blush on the apples of the cheeks makes the face more youthful; applying blush under the cheekbones slims the face and makes it appear drawn.

(continued from page 119)

ELIZABETH: They say I'm a cool and hip mom. They all seem to value my opinions and ask for advice on things all the time because they know I will offer my opinion without being judgmental. Even though I am first and foremost a mom, my girls are also my friends.

SCOTT: You stay very active. How do you keep up your energy?
ELIZABETH: I am a very energetic person by nature. I get up early, exercise, and begin my day. I always look at a new day as being an opportunity to begin another adventure and to discover something new. My trick is working with youngsters. I teach horseback riding to 4-H kids. I also substitute teach. Kids keep you thinking young. My grandson does that every day.

SCOTT: Do you normally wear a lot of makeup?
ELIZABETH: It depends on what I've got going on. For my usual routine, I use mineral veil for powder, put on a little blush, some eye makeup, and that's about it. It takes me about twenty minutes. I take a little longer to do my hair, because I use hot curlers.

(continued on page 122)

Elizabeth's Reaction
to Her Transformation

'Going into the day, I was very nervous because I thought, 'Oh my God, everyone's going to think I'm decrepit.' But everybody turned out to be so nice. I felt great about everything."

'I'm amazed at how Scott made me look. My first reaction was, 'I never thought I could look like this.' Looking at myself in the mirror, I felt extremely confident. The new hairstyle and the eyebrows—it's just amazing how those things make such a

(continued from page 121)

SCOTT: You have great skin. Do you do a lot for skin care?

ELIZABETH: I try to take care of my skin, yes. In the mornings when I take my shower, I scrub my face with one of those exfoliant cleansers, and then I put on my creams. I have three or four favourite creams I use and rotate: one with Retinol-A, one with DMAE (dimethylaminoethanol), one with peptides, and one with Alpha Hydroxy. In the evening, I do basically the same thing, but I use a heavier night cream.

SCOTT: When do you feel most confident?

ELIZABETH: I don't consider myself an overly confident person to begin with, but I think I feel best when I'm interacting with other people, making them laugh—when we're all enjoying ourselves. And on those days when my hair comes out good, which is rare!

difference. And making the eyes larger—I always thought I knew how to use makeup to enhance my eyes, but Scott taught me tricks that work even better. It just goes to show you can teach an old dog new tricks!"

"If I could describe myself before the makeover, it would probably be Elizabeth, the Sunday school teacher. But now I'd describe myself as Elizabeth, the sexy siren of the senior set!"

Evis:
Going Dramatic with Softer Colours

Evis has been one of my closest friends for years. She was born and raised in Albania, but she's now a film and television actress who has lived in Los Angeles for the past eight years. Evis also dates a rock star and could easily live the life of a wild child consisting of drinking, drugs, and frivolity that the industry is famous for. But she doesn't. She's disciplined, she has strong values, and she makes it a point to stay grounded.

In her life, as in her acting, Evis is fearless. That includes not being afraid to experiment with her appearance. In fact, I never quite know what she'll look like the next time I see her because she's always changing her hair colour. The day of her makeover, Evis came in with very dark hair and pink lips that, although dramatic, were too severe for her colouring and minimized her best features. I decided to warm up and balance her look. Now, instead of one feature, we focus in on a strikingly beautiful woman.

Scott + Evis Talk …

SCOTT: I see you've changed your hair colour again.

EVIS: You know me; I like to change it every six months, depending on my mood. People treat you differently depending on your hair colour. There really is that thing that when you're blonde, guys think you're a little ditzy. But they take you more seriously with dark hair. I had red hair for a period of time, too.

SCOTT: I remember. Is there anything else besides your hair colour that you would like to change about yourself?

EVIS: I'm not sure what I would change about myself. I'm kind of used to my face by now. If we're talking about other parts of the body? I'd say better boobs—subtle, not too big [laughs]. Is there a makeup to help with that?

SCOTT: If you could figure that out, you'd make lots of money! Let's talk about your beauty regimen. What do you do on a regular basis?

EVIS: In the morning I wash my face with cold water and then apply moisturizer and

(continued on page 127)

Creating Evis's Look

1

2

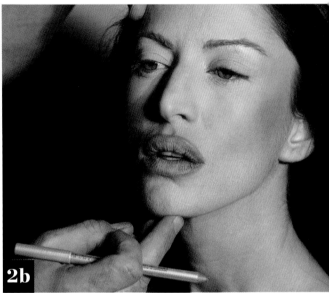

2b

Tip You can line your lips in one of two places:
• Just inside the lip line to soften fuller lips • Right on the border of the lip for normal to smaller lips I never recommend lining outside the border of the lip. Read that last statement again. I have a name for the look this kind of lining creates, but it's not appropriate to put in print, so I'll just call it clown mouth. Stay away from lining outside the lip. Stay away from clown mouth.

(continued from page 125)

Evis likes a dramatic look, so she tends to go for sharp contrasts in colouring. I wanted to show her how she could still create high drama with softer, warmer colours that draw out her own features, particularly her fantastic eyes.

1 Contouring, highlighting, and foundation

Evis doesn't like a lot of foundation, but I still wanted to warm up the colour of her skin without it feeling like too much makeup. As I did for Elizabeth, I chose to airbrush Evis's foundation, which in Evis's case would provide even coverage without feeling like heavy makeup.

With an airbrush, I applied a light beige foundation with a warm tone all over her face and neck. Evis has very pale skin, so I didn't want to go too dark with her foundation. Just adding this tiny bit of colour significantly warmed up her overall colouring. I used no highlighter or concealer on Evis. Instead, I let the lighter airbrush foundation suffice for the highlight.

2 Lips

Evis has really full, really beautiful lips, but the last thing I wanted to do was overemphasize them with lip lining, especially because I wanted to switch the focus from her lips to her extraordinary greenish-blue eyes. However, I still want to give the lips some definition. **(a)** Using a flesh-coloured lip liner, I lined just slightly inside the border of her lips. A colour any darker would have drawn more focus toward her lips, which I didn't want to do. **(b)** I finished off the lips with a peachy-coloured gloss.

an eye cream. And then at night I usually do a face scrub with an exfoliator. My skin is combination skin. I also exercise—not a lot, but a little bit of yoga and a little bit of cardio.

SCOTT: What else do you do to stay beautiful?
EVIS: Probably the biggest thing I do that makes a difference is I drink nothing but water, smoothies and juices—no soda, no coffee, and no alcohol. It's the best thing for my skin and body. And I stay out of the sun.

SCOTT: Do you follow a special diet, too?
EVIS: I eat pretty healthy, pretty much everything organic, including organic meat with no hormones. I eat vegetables, a lot of sushi, and I drink lots of water. My boyfriend says I eat a lot, so I think I have a very high metabolism.

SCOTT: You travel a lot. Is there anything you do differently for your skin when travelling?
EVIS: Yes, I apply extra moisturizer. And I don't usually wear foundation when I travel, because I like to let my skin breathe. I also drink a lot more water.

3a

3b

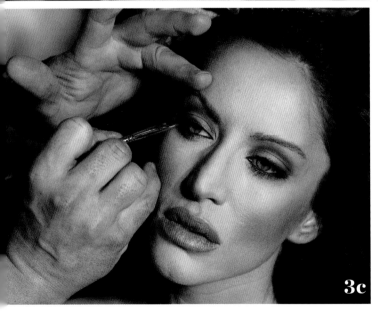

3c

Tip Using a warmer eye shadow for the base is a good idea if you also intend to use darker colours to create a "smoky" look. The warmer colour helps soften the look overall by blending the line between the darker and lighter sections of the eye.

3 Eyes

Evis has very pale greenish-blue eyes that are stunning—they deserve emphasis. When applying the eye shadow, I used different eye shadow brushes for each step for cleaner application. Using separate brushes is the best way to avoid mixing eye shadow colours in their cases. **(a)** Using a tapered eye shadow brush, I surrounded the eye with gold leaf eye shadow—putting it on the lid, in the crease, and under the eye—before laying in the darker colours. The purpose of this was not only to create warmth and bring out the blue in her eyes but also to unify the canvas, which allowed me to build up from there. **(b)** I then layered burgundy eye shadow over the gold eye shadow in the crease of the eye to create more dimension. **(c)** I also put this burgundy eye colour underneath the eye and in the outer corners. The reddish tone helped draw out the blue in Evis's pupils. **(d)** I used a brown Maybelline pencil to line inside of her upper and lower eyelids. **(e)** I completed the eye with some medium-density false eyelashes.

4 Cheeks

I wanted to go with very subtle blush on Evis's cheeks to keep the focus drawn toward her eyes. So, I used natural colours that simply warmed up her face without adding a lot of colour. **(a)** Moving the blush brush in a circular motion, I applied a cream peach-coloured blush to the apples of her cheeks. **(b)** With a separate bronzing brush, I lightly dusted loose bronzing powder on top of the blush to bring more warmth into the peachy tone. **(c)** I delicately applied a small amount of champagne shimmer highlight on top of the cheekbones.

Tip With shimmer highlight, a little bit goes a very long way for reflecting the light. So, be careful not to spill excess powder on other parts of your cheeks or face.

Evis's Reaction to Her Transformation

"Scott is not just another makeup artist; he's a real force of nature. I mean, look at the difference in me! He can transform a woman from regular to extraordinary. I've worked with Scott a few other times and I'm always impressed with how meticulous he is. The way he works is very, very thorough. But it's not just because of the way he applies the makeup. Scott also has a way of stripping away a person's insecurities during the process. That's a fierce makeover. I'm also excited about trying some of these new colours. Looking like I have a warmer skin tone changes me completely. And the reddish-browns he used definitely make my eyes stand out more; like they're a brighter bluish-green. Once again, Scott has taught me something new. I'm lucky to have a friend who's such a master of beauty."

Each of us
 has that right, that
possibility, to invent
ourselves daily.
If a person does not
invent herself,
 she will be invented.
—Maya Angelou

Sarah:
Applying Makeup for Natural, No-Makeup Beauty

Makeup doesn't always have to be about changing your look or creating drama. Sometimes less is definitely more. Sarah's face—with her French–Italian features and colouring—conjures up portraits from the neoclassical period. Her flawless skin gives her the option of using makeup to merely enhance her beauty for a natural, no-makeup look. But this kind of minimal look isn't achieved by simply walking out the door without makeup. Creating the illusion of "fresh and naturally beautiful" still requires a little time and effort. But as Sarah's transformation reveals, it can definitely be worth it. This look is just as relevant today as it was centuries ago.

Scott + Sarah Talk ...

SCOTT: How do you keep your skin looking so good?
SARAH: I've been lucky in that I've never really had skin problems. So, I've never had to do anything special. I wash my face in the morning and at night. Anything more than that, especially in New York weather, is too much. It dries my skin out like crazy. I wash my face with Murad Clarifying Cleanser, and then I put on a moisturizer right after. I just started moisturizing about a year ago, when I should've been doing it all along, but that has really, really changed my skin. Now that I moisturize in the morning and at night, I hardly ever break out.

SCOTT: Do you have to stick to a special diet to maintain your good skin?
SARAH: Well, I don't eat fried food. I love popcorn, but I also try to stay away from salty foods. I eat a lot of protein, like grilled fish and grilled chicken, and steamed vegetables. In the morning, I'll eat some fruit or some oatmeal. I drink coffee. But mostly I drink water. I recently stopped drinking

(continued on page 137)

Creating
Sarah's
Look

1a

1b

1c

2

The better your skin is, the more likely you'll be able to pull off the no-makeup look since it's really about taking healthy skin and making it look healthier. So, first make sure your skin is in the best possible shape—hydrated, with no significant marks or blemishes. (See "The Skinny on Skin" chapter for ways to maintain healthy skin.)

Instead of powder, I used oils and shimmers to highlight the top of Sarah's cheekbones and the end of her nose. This look isn't about using a lot of colour. In fact, I achieved this whole look using only three colours: wine-burgundy, champagne, and gold. I recommend using only berry and wine colours for this look, as they are the same colours found in nature.

1 Contouring, highlighting, and foundation

Sarah already has healthy, glowing skin, so I used cream-based products for her contouring, highlighting, and foundation. **(a)** Using a goat hair brush, I applied contouring (dark) foundation: • Underneath the cheekbones • On the sides of the nose • At the inner eye where the bridge of the nose meets the brow bone • At the temples **(b)** Using a concealer brush, I brought out all her bones using highlights and shimmery creams. I applied the highlighting (light) concealer: • Underneath the eyes • On top of the cheekbones • Underneath the eyebrows • On the bridge of the nose • At the centre of the chin • In the centre of the forehead **(c)** Using a separate goat hair brush, I applied a foundation that matched her skin colouring on top of the contouring and highlighting. I blended in a circular motion with a very light touch for a flawless finish.

2 Setting the look

Before adding translucent powder, I wanted to absorb any excess makeup and push it into the skin so that it blended with her natural oils. **(a)** I placed a makeup sponge in the centre of a tissue. I then twisted the tissue around the sponge, as though I were wrapping a Hershey's kiss. **(b)** I lightly dabbed the tissue-sponge onto her skin. **(c)** I then applied a light dusting of translucent powder in the T-zone (chin, bridge of the nose, forehead, and underneath the eyes) to remove excess shine.

For the rest of the process I used nothing but cream-based makeup, which is very close to the consistency of lipstick. In fact, I've been known to achieve a very similar look with nothing but one tube of lipstick!

(continued from page 135)

as much alcohol as I used to. On the weekends, I'll go out and have a drink, but otherwise, hardly ever. I also drink a Diet Coke from time to time. My dad is an orthodontist, so growing up it was always "no soft drinks in the house, it's so bad for your teeth." So, we'd have to sneak them!

SCOTT: And how about exercise?
SARAH: I've been getting into Pilates and yoga two or three times a week. And I jog.

SCOTT: Do you like to wear a lot of makeup?
SARAH: I like to experiment when I go out, so I'll do smoky eyes or some crazy colours but still try to be fairly natural with it. I have roommates who take hours to get ready, but they are so naturally beautiful already. I don't understand why they need to do all the things they do to themselves.

SCOTT: How would you describe your everyday fashion style?

(continued on page 139)

An important part of the
NO-MAKEUP, RADIANT SKIN LOOK
is creating healthy,
flush coloured cheeks.

Tip When searching for a cream highlighter for your cheekbones, look for shimmery champagne colours, if you're Caucasian. If you're dark-skinned, the highlighter should have a warm, copper
tone to it.

Tip Use a light touch during application. Again, you want the look of minimal makeup.

(continued from page 137)

3 Cheeks

An important part of the no-makeup, radiant skin look is creating healthy, flush coloured cheeks. **(a)** Using my fingers, I applied to the apples of her cheeks a wine-coloured cream blush that was the same colour I would be using on her lips. **(b)** Using a blush brush, I blended this colour into the shimmery highlight cream, so there would be no separation between these two colours.

4 Eyes

For Sarah's eyes, I simply wanted to add a small bit of colour to her lids for a bit of dimension. **(a)** I put a gold cream across the whole lid. **(b)** I then applied champagne-coloured highlighter just under the brow bone. I put no mascara on Sarah; however, if you want mascara with this kind of minimal look, here's what I recommend: **(a)** Curl your lashes with your eyelash curler. **(b)** Wipe most of the mascara off the wand with a tissue, so there's a minimal amount on the brush. **(c)** Rub the end of the mascara wand with the tips of your index finger and thumb to stain them with some colour. *Note: Clean fingers will ensure you don't get any bacteria on the wand.* **(d)** Apply the mascara on your lashes using your fingers, instead of the mascara brush. This will give a "tint" of colour on the lashes, without looking like you've applied mascara.

5 Lips

The trick to creating lips that look like they're naturally flushed is to use a stain that's slightly darker than your natural lip colour. This gives the impression that the lips are flush and healthy. You don't want to use any kind of gloss or frosted colour that looks artificial or heavily covers the lip. **(a)** I first wanted to get the blood flowing to Sarah's lips. So, with a small, natural-bristle brush I brushed some lip balm lightly, back and forth, on both the top and bottom lips. This helps plump the lips as well as gets rid of any dead skin. **(b)** With my finger, I then applied the same cream cheek-coloured stain on Sarah's lips that I used on the apples of her cheeks.

SARAH: I wear a lot of my boyfriend's clothes—so, boyish and edgy.

SCOTT: What do you like to do outside of modelling?
SARAH: I love to read and write. I read all sorts of different things. And I write a lot. I eventually plan on going back to school for creative writing. I wrote for my hometown newspaper in Mississippi, USA when I was in seventh and eigth grade. So ever since then, I've always wanted to write for magazines about beauty and skin care.

SCOTT: Do you have any kind of life philosophy?
SARAH: I feel that whatever good, positive energy you put out into the world, that's what will come back to you. And I think it helps to be open to things and for making new friends all the time. What's the point of being negative?

Sarah's Reaction
to Her Transformation

'The result was beautiful. Scott made my skin literally glow. It was funny, because I told him in the beginning that I loved the natural look the best, and generally that I like to keep that the goal when doing my own makeup. So, I was so excited to see how he would do the no-makeup look. He didn't even use mascara. That's about as natural as it gets!"

"Before Scott, I would use a little bit of eyeliner on my top lids only, but since he showed me how I can make my skin look better while using less makeup, I realized that using dark eyeliner was actually making my face look older in a way. So, I definitely don't do that anymore. I really feel the new techniques give me a fresher, younger look."

The Skinny on Skin

In many ways, this chapter on skin should precede all the others, because there's really nothing more important than healthy, radiant skin when it comes to beauty. It's the canvas on which a look is created. Having bad skin is like starting with a canvas that's torn or stained—you spend your whole time working around and covering blemishes. Fortunately, today it's easier than it used to be to have great skin. And that's what this chapter is about: how to give your skin some loving so that it glows.

People often wonder why they don't look as good as many celebrities. They attribute a star's good looks to something they can't personally achieve themselves. I hear it all the time: "Star X must have been born with good genes" or "The gods blessed Star Y when they made her." Well, here's the inside scoop: These so-called natural beauties work at it. Their beauty, in large part, is due to how they take care of their bodies. They make sure to exercise on a regular basis, they make healthy food choices, and they put long-term gain ahead of short-term gratification. And when they indulge every now and then—which they do because they're only human—they do what it takes to make up for it.

Here's some tough love: You can't expect to look beautiful if you don't put some effort into it.

I'd like to introduce my good friend, Eva Cwynar, M.D., or Dr. Eva, as she's affectionately known by her clients. Dr. Eva is a world-renowned endocrinologist, metabolic medicine specialist, and internist practicing in Beverly Hills, California. She is on the faculty at Cedars-Sinai Medical Centre and serves as an assistant clinical professor of medicine at UCLA.

Scott: Dr. Eva, what would you advise people in taking care of their skin?

Dr. Eva: I'd say there are a couple of things that can make a huge difference to the health of your skin. The first is to Vita-Mineralize. The best way to get vitamins and minerals is by eating a balanced, colourful diet of fruits and veggies and by taking your supplements. Vitamins and minerals are catalysts. Once they're absorbed into your body, they go to work setting off a chain reaction in other parts of your body to produce the necessary elements we need to function. It's as if you are treating your internal system to a good workout. Much like a good trainer, they make sure your body gets what it needs to look your very best and ensure everything's working properly on a molecular level. Most importantly, these food sources contain the antioxidants our body needs to fight those nasty little things called free radicals.

Scott: Let's take a moment to talk about those wicked free radicals and the effect they have on our skin. What can you tell us about them?

Dr. Eva: Free radicals, which are unstable molecules, are produced in our bodies as a result of many things: over-exposure to UVA rays, radiation, smoking, environmental pollutants, alcohol, injury, ageing, strenuous exercise, and chronic disease. Once these free radicals form and begin attacking our bodies, they can do some real damage...to our skin, our heart, and our other organs. In general, they weaken the immune system and make a person more susceptible to the development of cardiovascular diseases and even cancer. So you want to make sure you're getting plenty of antioxidants to counteract these malicious free radicals.

Another thing you can do for your skin is GET PLENTY OF PROTEIN.
—Dr. Eva

Antioxidants exist as vitamins (namely A, C and E), enzymes, and other compounds in foods.

Scott: It's a pretty simple equation: what you put in your body gets reflected on how you look on the outside.

Dr. Eva: That's a great way to put it. Another thing you can do for your skin is get plenty of protein. Protein is the natural building block for healthy collagen, and as we all know, collagen keeps your skin firm and toned...kind of like a yoga class for your skin!

Scott: Firm and tone with protein, ladies!

Dr. Eva: One last, very important thing I would like to mention: Provide some TLC with EFAs. Essential fatty acids (EFAs) are as essential to your diet as vitamins. They provide tender, loving care for your skin as well as your arteries and heart. They're even great for relieving PMS and monthly breast pain. EFAs cannot be produced in from within our body, so we must include them in our diet. There are two important families of EFAs: Omega 6s found in plant oils, nuts, seeds, and soybeans and Omega 3s found in cold water fish, cod liver oil, and flax seed.

Omega 6s can also be taken in the form of supplements. Just be sure to look for Omega 6 supplements that have been purified and are mercury-free. There are many cheap non-purified Omega 6 supplements out there which can lead to mercury toxicity.

So whether you enjoy a handful of nuts, a nice fish dinner, or take your Omega 6s in the form of supplements, just make sure you regularly lubricate your skin with EFAs.

Scott: We all know a little lubrication can go a very long way...Thank you, Dr. Eva!

How to Give Your Skin Some Loving

Here are some things you can do that will make the most difference to the health of your skin.

Moisturize, Moisturize, Moisturize

No doubt you've heard this many times. Think of moisturizing as adding a protective sealant to your skin that prevents water from escaping. Some moisturizers even gradually release water into the skin. Surprisingly, it is not dry skin itself that causes wrinkles; rather, it's the cell damage that occurs deeper beneath the skin's surface that causes skin to break down and form wrinkles. Skin tends to get drier as you age, and it becomes much more susceptible to damage and infection. So, counteracting dry skin by moisturizing really does help to slow down the ageing process! Also, if you have problem areas with extra-dry skin, seek out heavier creams and apply them nightly.

Moisturize from Within

Drink water for a better complexion. The more you drink, the better your skin will be. Some people will debate this direct correlation, but the facts are that drinking water, just like exercising, helps to increase blood flow. And as with exercise, better circulation is better for the skin. Drinking water also helps to flush toxins out of the body, and we know toxins are bad for skin. Toxins lead to blemishes. So, fewer toxins equal fewer blemishes, which equates to smoother, prettier skin! How much water do you need? Just pay attention to your body; it will tell you when you need water. If your lips are parched or your nose is itchy and dry or you're simply thirsty, you need more water—not soda, water!

Get Off That Couch

Most people think of exercise as a way to cut calories or get rid of fat or strengthen their muscles. But it's also terrific for your skin. Whenever you improve your circulation, you improve your skin since healthy, glowing skin depends on good blood flow. Also, sweating during exercise is one of the most natural ways to get rid of those terrible toxins.

FAKE IT, DON'T BAKE IT

There are a lot of things women fake— fake boobs, fake hair, or a fake nose. Why stop there when you can go for the fake tan? Too much exposure to the sun makes you look like an old Gucci bag. Unsexy! This is why I created Body Bling and other self tanners, so you can get a gorgeous tan without risking overexposure to those nasty UVA rays.

Restore with Sleep

They call it "beauty sleep" for a reason. Sleep and beauty really are interrelated. Everything regenerates when you sleep. Your mind renews, your cells renew, and your skin renews. I like to believe that when I'm sleeping, a housekeeper comes in and tidies up, making the bed and ironing out my wrinkles and removing the toxins from the night before. She restores the whole house before I have to get up and at it the next morning.

Body builders also understand the importance of restorative sleep. Their first rule of thumb is to get plenty of sleep after a hard workout. They know they won't see any improvement in their muscles until they've slept and given their muscles time to rebuild. So, never feel guilty about sneaking a nap or sleeping in. If you feel tired, it's your body telling you it needs time

to repair. You'll be rewarded with healthier skin when you wake up!

Shed the Dead (Skin)

It's important to exfoliate twice a month to remove the dead cells on the top layer of your skin. Dead skin is the chief reason for skin appearing dull and dry, so when you exfoliate, you immediately gain a more youthful luster to your skin. The increased blood flow that results from invigorated skin also helps stimulate collagen growth. Dead skin also tends to block pores and trap bacteria, so regular exfoliation can also help control acne. But remember: Do not exfoliate more than twice a month. Overexfoliation can be damaging to your skin; if you begin to strip away healthy cells in addition to the dead cells, this can lead to an outbreak of acne. The best indication that you're overexfoliating is if your skin feels irritated or you see increased redness. Your skin should be pleasantly tingly, not burning , after exfoliating.

Create Your Own Tropical Paradise

You don't have to go to the tropics to achieve the benefits that humidity and moisture provide to your skin. You can create your own tropical paradise with a humidifier and a few plants. Or you can invest in a miniature fountain, which is a more aesthetically pleasing humidifier. Whatever you buy, the point is to moisten the air with H_2O. This is particularly important in the winter when the dry air from heaters sucks the moisture from your skin. Also, did you know that your skin dehydrates when your sleep? And dehydration causes skin to wrinkle and sag. See where I'm going with this? So, if you don't want to run your humidifier all the time, use it only at night. Placing some plants around is also nice, not only because they liven up your surroundings (quite literally) but also because research has shown that plants help you feel more relaxed and prompt you to breathe deeper, allowing more oxygen to enter your system. Plants also help to remove chemicals—toxins— from the air.

Indulge in a Night of Beauty

I'm all about pampering with facials, massages, and whatnot. But I don't believe it has to cost a mint. Give yourself a break both physically and financially by staying home one night a month to indulge in a "night of beauty." Luxuriate in a hot bath filled with body oils while drinking a seltzer with mint. Give yourself a home facial. Have some good sex or fanta- size about good sex. It's all about letting go of the tension and thoroughly relaxing so that you breathe deep and easy. The increased oxygen in your blood is a wonderful boost for your skin.

The best news is that our skin cells are constantly regenerating. So if you have problem skin or you've damaged your skin, there are many, many things you can do, starting today, to have better skin. You can minimize skin damage or get rid of it altogether, thanks to technological advances in skin care, whether they be creams, injections or more advanced treatments.

Home Facial Recipe

To give yourself a facial, follow these steps: **(1)** Put on some relaxing music. **(2)** Boil some water in a covered quart-size pot, with or without chamomile herbs. **(3)** While you're waiting for the water to boil, cleanse your face and then grab a very large towel or blanket. **(4)** When the water comes to a boil, remove the pot from the stove and place it somewhere where you can sit comfortably with your face leaning over it. (You can also stand at the stove, but it's less comfortable.) **(5)** Remove the lid and let some of the initial steam escape before putting your face into the steam. **(6)** Cover your head and the pot with the blanket or towel. **(7)** Sit in your tent of steam and breathe deeply for seven to ten minutes. **(8)** Pat your face dry, apply a moisturizing mask, and leave it on for fifteen minutes. **(9)** Remove the mask with cool water. **(10)** Follow with a good moisturizer. Voilà! You now have happier, suppler skin!

Skin Damage and How You Can Avoid It

My good friend Dr. Jessica Wu is considered one of the top skin doctors in the United States. Recently, I sat down with Dr. Wu—along with Maureen Kornowa and her daughter, Marley, whom I had met at the annual Make a Wish Charity—to discuss the importance of caring for your skin.

SCOTT: How does a person know when to seek out a skin specialist?

DR. WU: As soon as something starts to bother you, then you should visit a doctor. That's not to say some people aren't deluded sometimes. I've had sixteen- and seventeen-year-olds who believe they have a frown line and come in for a Botox injection. I send them home. But the general rule of thumb is, when something starts to bother you, it's time to see a dermatologist. And you may not need an injection or laser; you may simply need a topical Retin-A cream or a topical antioxidant. But there are definitely things we can do to help improve what you have as well as prevent further lines from appearing.

SCOTT: So, since everyone can't fly to Los Angeles and get an appointment with the fabulous Dr. Wu, how does someone go about finding a top dermatologist?

DR. WU: One of the best places to start is with your regular doctor. Or you can usually get a good referral from your makeup artist or your facialist or even your hairstylist because these people are in the business of beauty and appearance. A lot of times, their clients will talk about a good or bad experience if they've had one, so they will know someone who has a reputation for doing good work.

SCOTT: In other words, don't pick your doctor out of the yellow pages and certainly not from one of those late night television commercials. How often do you recommend people see a dermatologist?

DR. WU: I strongly recommend people come in once a year, and in the course of doing a mole examination, we'll talk about other things. For example, people will notice a lot of sun damage on their cheeks that they want to clear up. Or they have acne concerns.

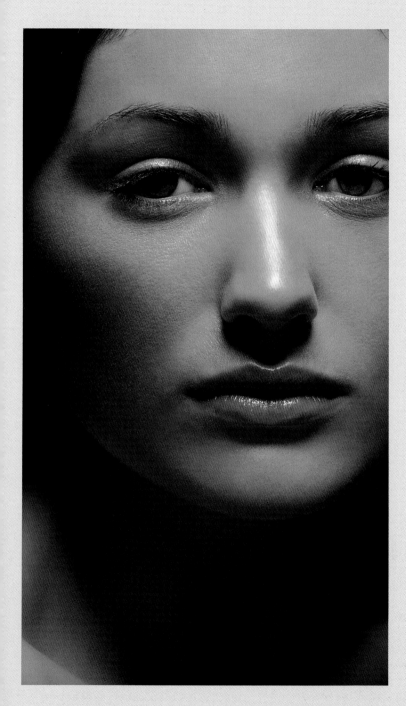

MAKEUP sits
better on skin
that isn't
sun damaged.

SCOTT: I think makeup sits better on skin that isn't sun damaged. The skin is easier to cover when you have an even skin tone and when you're skin's softer, more supple. The makeup looks more like it's a part of your skin, not like it's sitting on top.

DR. WU: Yes, I think your job is much easier when someone has good skin versus when someone comes in and they're all weather-beaten.

SCOTT: What are your thoughts about sun block?

DR. WU: I recommend using a lotion with an SPF of at least 30. And just as important as the SPF when looking for ingredients is that the product protects against UVA rays. UVAs are the ageing rays. The SPF number only tells you how good the product is at protecting you from burning. When I was creating my skin-care line in the lab, the list of ingredients for SPF was overwhelming. I cut through all of those ingredients and realized that the three key ingredients for skin-care protection are zinc, titanium, or mexoryl, so make sure you're getting a product that includes at least one of these.

The other point I want to make is that a lot of my patients come in because their makeup artist notices a suspicious spot. These people are right there, up in their faces. Or their massage therapists or their facialists notice things. That's definitely the reason why it's good to have relationships with these other beauty professionals. So, listen when your makeup artist notices something or your hairstylist tells you there's something in your scalp. Listen to them.

SCOTT: That's true. People should check their scalp and between their toes. Doctors don't usually do that. And a lot of dermatologists don't check between the toes. I've never been to anybody but you, Jessica, who has checked between my toes.

DR. WU: It's a good idea to check everywhere for anything that wasn't there before.

SCOTT: Since we're talking about noticing things on your skin, we've got to address the issue of skin cancer. Skin care isn't just about beauty, it's also about protecting yourself and being smart about taking care of your skin, so you don't run the risk of getting skin

The three key ingredients for **SKIN-CARE PROTECTION** are zinc, titanium, *or* mexoryl.

cancer. And that's where Maureen and Marley come in. You look at their photo and you see two beautiful people who just seem to glow. But what you don't see is that Marley is a seventeen-year-old girl dealing with Stage 3 melanoma, the deadliest form of skin cancer. And this is something Marley and her mother and father have been dealing with over the past year.

MAUREEN: It's been a challenging year, to say the least.

SCOTT: Having lost my thirty-year-old brother to melanoma two years ago, I understand much of what you've been going through. Cancer moves in, and you've got a new member of the family, and you want them to leave already.

MARLEY: It's like a third person in the room.

MAUREEN: In the past year, we've been on a journey that began the day Marley received her diagnosis of Stage 3 cancer. Even though the journey had a lot of setbacks and detours in the beginning and some ugly news, Marley, in particular, hit that road on that journey with perseverance and laughter. We've found cancer humorous because it made the bad days a little bit easier. We thought, "Oh, if we're going to

sit here and go through this, we're going to have some fun doing it."

MARLEY: I named my pickline "Fiero" from the play Wicked, because Fiero was kind of sweet, and we put a scarf on it and I took Fiero to homecoming. We laugh at stuff like that.

SCOTT: You have to poke fun at it, because otherwise it starts beating you. It's good; it's healthy to play around with it.

MAUREEN: There are really two ways to approach life: Let it get you and curl up and die, or hold your head up high and laugh and do what's got to be done. With Marley, there was never any question which road it was going to be. From day one, she held her head high.

MARLEY: I believe there's a reason I have cancer. And part of the reason is cancer has brought my family closer. It has taught me things and taught us about being a family. I thank cancer for that.

SCOTT: And that's my attraction to you. You both possess such grace and dignity under such difficult circumstances. That personifies beauty for me. It's that inner strength and that inner beauty that just radiates, and it shows in your

In general, everyone should get their skin CHECKED ONCE A YEAR regardless of their age.

photograph. I saw it the day I met you. Out of all those people in the room, I was automatically drawn to you guys. And you don't run across that every day.

MAUREEN: Having gone through this experience with Marley's cancer, I would say that I have learned that you've got to get yourself checked once a year by a dermatologist, regardless of your age. I think there's a common misconception out there among the general populace that you shouldn't start getting your skin checked until you're older. But the truth is that melanoma is becoming more and more prevalent in younger people. You're not too young to have a deadly skin disease.

DR. WU: That's right. In general, everyone should get their skin checked once a year regardless of their age. Just like you get your blood pressure checked or your cholesterol checked or women do their mammograms or pelvic exams once a year, they should also get their skin checked. That's because skin cancer is one of the most preventable cancers. I tell patients, "If you can see it, then you can remove it early enough; it's curable." The problem comes up when people think that just because

it's on your skin and not internal, it's not really a problem. So, they ignore it. My response to that is, while it may not hurt you initially or you may not feel pain initially, if you wait too long it can travel internally and be potentially devastating.

So, the bottom line is everyone should get their skin checked once a year and even more frequently— every six months—if you have a history of skin cancer in your family, if the doctors ever found anything suspicious on you, and especially if you were sunburned as a child. We know that blistering sunburns and the use of tanning beds increase your risk. So, if you've had sunburns or used a tanning bed, you should start in your teens and twenties.

SCOTT: Tanning beds are shaped like a coffin for a reason.
DR. WU: So true.
SCOTT: And I'm guilty of being a tanner myself. But I've been educated through things like my brother's death and through not wanting to age. The work that you and I have done to reverse the damage has been enlightening, to say the least. Don't risk it by baking yourself!
MAUREEN: I want to point out that Marley is not someone who used

a tanning bed or who fried herself by laying out in the sun. She's an average, healthy teenager. Doctors now believe there may be a genetic connection, something hereditary. Although that wasn't even the case in our family—no one else in our families had ever had cancer. So, have your young kids checked once a year, period.

SCOTT: When faced with such a difficult, all-consuming challenge, the question becomes, how are you going to deal with it? In spite of your condition, Marley, you are still a beautiful young woman with a positive attitude and enough courage not only to get up and speak in front of hundreds of people, but to speak about something as personal as your cancer.

MARLEY: Thanks. I just believe it's what I'm supposed to do.

SCOTT: Well, you're a real inspiration to all of us.

MAUREEN: You can see why I'm so proud. And she always makes the point when she speaks: Don't underestimate skin cancer.

DR. WU: That's right, which is why it's important to do your own self-examinations every now and then.

SCOTT: What should people look for?

DR. WU: Look for any kind of change. That's why it's important to check your skin yourself once a month because as your doctor whom you see only once a year I'm not going to know what's changing. My job is to give you a baseline when you come in once a year, and your job is once a month or so to take a look at yourself and see if there are any changes. Is anything growing? Is it getting darker? Does anything itch or bleed? Do you have a sore that won't go away? If any of these things are happening, then you need to bring it to the doctor's attention.

SCOTT: Some great advice. And I don't want to forget to mention that Jessica has created an incredible line of skin-care products. So, check 'em out on her website, www.DrJessicaWu.com.

DR. WU: Thanks, Scott.

BEAUTY IS more about being a good person and the way you carry yourself rather than your outside looks.

SCOTT: Let's end with everyone's thoughts on becoming your most beautiful self.

DR. WU: I think it all starts with beautiful skin because your skin is what you present to the world. Your skin, your face, your hair—it's all on display. Also important is confidence. Whenever you make me up, Scott, you make me feel so confident. You can't inject that, you can't take a pill for that, but having confidence is beautiful.

MARLEY: Beauty is more about being a good person and the way you carry yourself rather than your outside looks.

MAUREEN: I would agree completely with my beautiful daughter. So now you're all fully aware that taking care of your skin is serious stuff. You can't expect to have great skin unless you make wise, skin-sensitive choices. All of the beautiful women in this book are a testament to that. Be sure to check out their skin-care regimens, including their approach to diet and exercise. And while we haven't yet figured out how to reverse the ageing process, we have identified plenty of things within our control that can not only slow down the ageing process, but also enhance the health of our skin overall.

The best part is, in addition to looking healthier and learning about better makeup application, having great skin is also an amazing confidence booster. And that's perhaps the most important ingredient for becoming the best possible version of your sassy self!

Transformations

Irina:
Using Bronzer and Highlights to Create a Sun-Kissed Glow

Scott + Irina Talk ...

There's no denying the fact that Irina is a sexy woman. You feel her sensuality the moment she walks in the room. And that's why she's the current Guess jeans model—because she knows how to sell adventurous sex. Irina has entered the ranks of supermodels Claudia Schiffer, Anna Nicole Smith, and Eva Herzigova. But what people don't see when looking at her print image is that in addition to her apparent beauty and sex appeal Irina also has an incredibly goofy side. She and I have worked together on several different ad campaigns, and whenever we get together, much laughter is involved. She's a woman who is comfortable in her own skin—whether her clothes are on or off—and she's a great example of someone who is aware of who she is and what her power is. And that's what this book is about: the power of owning your beauty.

Scott + Irina Talk ...

SCOTT: When modelling for products like Guess jeans and lingerie, you usually have to show a lot of skin. Are you ever uncomfortable in front of the camera being so bare?

IRINA: Actually, I know that for some models, showing skin is a bit hard, but I love to work out, so I feel good about my body. Especially when I have sexy makeup and big hair: It gives me something for the shoot and helps bring something to the picture. And people are usually looking more at the face and hair than at your clothing (or lack of). So no, I don't ever feel shy or uncomfortable in front of the camera.

SCOTT: How do you stay in such good shape?

IRINA: I work out with my trainer about three to four times a week. He has a special program for me where I don't use weights. I use the weight of my body or I use very light weights, like books. I don't have any particular diet. I love to eat. I eat cake and this kind of high calorie food all the time. I think it's all about

(continued on page 163)

Creating Irina's Look

 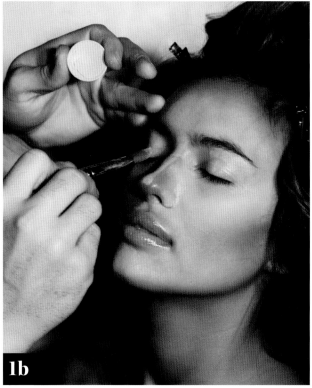

1a **1b**

Tip You can put some contouring underneath the tip of the nose, to give the illusion of shortening the nose.

In my mind, Irina is a cross between a James Bond girl and Japanese anime. There's something fantastical about her. I didn't want to change Irina's look as much as I wanted to create a look worthy of an Olivia de Berardinis pin-up!

....

1 Contouring, concealer, and foundation

Even though I was going for a warm, tanned look for Irina, I still needed to make sure her face had dimension and light. Looking tan isn't achieved simply by putting on a darker shade of foundation on the face. Using only one colour has the effect of flattening out the face and making it look too dark. A facial tan still requires adding brightness and depth underneath the foundation first. **(a)** Using light strokes and a goat hair brush, I applied contouring (dark) cream: • Underneath the jaw line • Underneath the cheekbones • Down the sides of the nose • Underneath the tip of the nose • At the inner eye where the bridge of the nose meets the brow bone • At the top of the forehead **(b)** With shorter brushstrokes, I used a concealer brush and applied highlighting (light) concealer: • Under the eyes • Down the tip of the nose • In the middle of the forehead • At the centre of the chin • On the brow bone • Covering the eye (except at the inner eye where I wanted to keep some depth) **(c)** I wanted to give Irina a warm, tanned appearance, so I applied Body Bling all over her body. You can see how much lighter the face is than the body, so the foundation is about marrying the face and body together. **(d)** I used a separate goat hair brush and applyied a light caramel-coloured foundation on her face that was one shade lighter than the colour of her body but one shade darker than her natural skin tone. I moved the brush in small circles to delicately blend on top of the contouring and highlighting. *Remember: Anytime you're building your face to match your body, you want to do it in layers so that your face doesn't come out looking too dark. Remember to keep more light in the centre of your face and use the bronzing foundation more around the outside.*

(continued from page 161)

how you eat, of course, but it's also about balancing. If you love to eat, you have to work out so your body will still look great.

SCOTT: What do you think is your best trait?
IRINA: I think that if I really, really, really want something, I can get it. It doesn't matter what it is, I'm going to find a way to get it. I can push myself. For me, it's never about wanting something and just dreaming about it; it's about taking the steps to get there. Many people, if something goes wrong, they'll give up. If I don't succeed, I can look at it a different way and find another way to approach it.

SCOTT: And your worst trait?
IRINA: Sometimes I can be very, very lazy. Let's say it's raining. I can talk myself out of going somewhere. But then, ten minutes later, I say, "No, I have to go." Also, I can be very moody. Just sometimes, but it's something I would like to get better about.

SCOTT: What are your interests outside of modelling?
IRINA: Before modelling, I went to music school for seven years, and I sang in

(continued on page 165)

2 **4a**

4b **4c**

4d

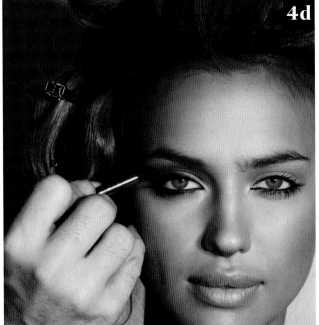

Tip: Always approach blush in a very soft way, layering little by little. You can always add more, but it's very hard to remove without washing your face.

2 Cheeks

I wanted to give Irina's cheeks some colour without being too overpowering. To get just the right shade, I blended two blushes together as follows. **(a)** I applied a punchy, vibrant pink cream blush to the apples of her cheeks, moving the blush brush in a circular motion. **(b)** Using a different blush brush, I layered a very vibrant peach cream blush on top of the pink, also blending in circles for a smooth, seamless finish. **(c)** To help give her cheeks more definition, I applied a very light dusting of 24-Carat Bronze highlighter on the tops of her cheekbones as well as on the apples of her cheeks for a fine sheen.

4 Eyes

To accentuate Irina's gray-green eyes, I created a smokier look by surrounding her eyes with deep rich colour. **(a)** I lined the inner rim of her upper and lower lids with a black Maybelline eye pencil. **(b)** I curled her lashes and used tons of black mascara. **(c)** I surrounded her eyes with a rich chocolate-brown eye shadow. I applied it into the crease, above the crease, and underneath the eye. **(d)** With a different eye shadow brush, I went over the top of the brown eye shadow with a black eye shadow to create a smoky effect. The black by itself would've been too harsh, so I muted it by first applying the chocolate brown. **(e)** Finally, I added lots of individual false eyelashes on her upper lid.

Tip The trick with smoky eyes, like blush, is to start slow and layer up. You can always add more if necessary

.

3 Setting the look

With a large powder brush, I applied a warm beige loose powder all over the face to set the look as well as to add a warm glow.

(continued from page 163)

a choir. I was one of the soloists for two years. I was a bass because I have this kind of voice [she speaks very low]. My mom is a pianist, so when I was I kid, we had a piano, and I always played with my sister.

SCOTT: Do you still sing?
IRINA: Just when I take a shower. I miss it. But it's a very hard career. With singing, you have to really be into it and you don't have much time for anything else. You can't drink cold drinks, you can't drink hot drinks, and you can't eat spicy food because all these things change your voice. And I'm enjoying the modelling now.

SCOTT: You're a hot model these days, working all the time. What do you think it takes to stay competitive in the industry?
IRINA: I think you have to always be yourself. There are always so many people around and other models, so you have to be really natural. And of course, you have to be very strong and not let the pressure get to you. I can't say that I'm better than another model. I just try to be myself and I really like what I do. It also helps to stay positive, which is easier when you enjoy what you're doing.

(continued on page 167)

5 Eyebrows

Get that boar's hair eyebrow brush ready, it's time to do some eyebrows. Irina already had nicely shaped brows, so I merely wanted to make them bushier. There's something sexy about a very natural, unmanicured look to the brow.

I sprayed some hairspray onto the brush and then brushed it through the eyebrows in an upward motion.

6 Lips

Irina has nice full lips, so I didn't need to do any lining. **(a)** Her lips were a little dry, so I brushed the lips with some lip balm and a boar's hair bristle brush to slough off the dead skin and plump up the lips. **(b)** For colour, I applied a muted berry-coloured cream blush very sparingly with my fingers to mimic the colour of her lips.

(continued from page 165)

SCOTT: Do you feel hair and makeup enhance your sexuality?
IRINA: I would say it makes me feel more comfortable, sexier, and of course, I love to wear makeup and have my hair styled. But for my normal, everyday life, I never use makeup. I don't even buy mascara. But I really love to see makeup and hair done on me. For every woman, when her makeup is done and her hair is beautiful, she feels sexier. If I had someone who could do it for me, I would love to do it every night!

Tip Bushy brows are great for smoky eyes because they give the brows a softer, airier feel by breaking up the density of the brow, which matches the softness of the smoky eye.

Irina's Reaction to Her Transformation

"Scott really works like an artist—the way he's using his brushes and his product. I think when he sees the person with whom he's going to work, he gets an image in his head and he creates the look he sees on you, like he is creating a painting. I wouldn't say he changed my face, even though he could if he wanted to. Scott wants you to look the same, only more gorgeous. He wants it to look natural, so he made me beautiful by enhancing what I already have."

"Scott also has great energy. When it comes to makeup artists, you want the people who touch your skin to have a great energy and to be fun and easygoing. Scott is one of these kinds of people, which is very rare. Also, what I love about his makeup is when he's finished, you look healthy. Some makeup can make you look old. But his product is very light, which is good for the skin. With Scott, he really made my face glow, but he also made me feel very sexy just by the way he made me feel so beautiful."

Sonia:
Going Soft and Sexy with Shimmer Highlights

Sonia possesses a remarkable inner strength which compliments her strong, dark features. Originally from New Delhi, India, Sonia has a quiet confidence that allows her to talk easily and without conceit about herself and her approach to beauty. She starts each day with her yoga practice and peppers her conversation with phrases like "Something I deeply follow" and "I strongly believe." She seems at peace with herself and her place in the world.

Sonia also thinks like an entrepreneur. When I asked her about her skin-care regimen, Sonia told me she uses a special mask that was her own secret recipe. She wouldn't tell anyone what was in it because she plans to eventually mass market it herself. And I believe she will. Inspired by the book *The Alchemist*, by Brazilian author Paulo Coelho, Sonia states matter-of-factly that "if you want something, and you work towards it, the whole universe comes together to bring it to you."

Sonia's eyebrows are a dominant facial feature. I knew I had to start there because she had crazy brows: One was straight and the other was arched.

Scott + Sonia Talk ...

SCOTT: Who's plucking your eyebrows?
SONIA: Some random Indian chick off Newark Avenue [meaning herself].

SCOTT: Well, she has to be stopped. They're two different shapes.
SONIA: I know.

SCOTT: You have a very dark, thick brow, so we need to talk about how to maintain them, without plucking. I recommend using an eyebrow razor.
SONIA: Where do you get one of those?

SCOTT: You can get them at any chemist's. It's also good for any other kinds of facial hair. So, I'm first going to clean up those brows because I want the focus to be on your eyes.
SONIA: I like my eyes, except in the morning when they are puffy. And I like my cheekbones.

(continued on page 173)

Creating Sonia's Look

1

2a

2b

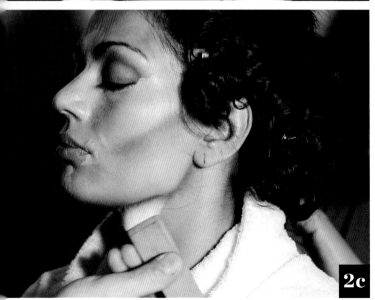

2c

Tip Yellow concealer cancels out the darkness in darker skin tones better than white or beige-coloured concealer, which tends to turn gray-blue on darker skin.

Sonia's beautiful dark features and strong jaw line give her a harder look. I wanted to soften her up for a more sensual, feminine appearance.

(continued from page 171)

SCOTT: Your eyes and cheekbones are your strongest area. You also have a pretty mouth, but that shouldn't be the main focus.

SONIA: I have a very square jaw line.

SCOTT: Yes, it's strong and gives you an angular look, so we're going to do things to soften it. Soft is more sensual, sexier. And you have the body to pull it off. What do you do for diet and exercise?

SONIA: Exercise is something I'm strict about because I believe it is very important to have discipline in your life. I work out four times a week. And I love doing sit-ups. I often compete with some cops who live in my building to see who can do more sit-ups. Other than that, I walk outside. I prefer to be out in nature. Weekday mornings, I also do yoga. It helps to release any negativity, so I start my day with clean, positive energy.

(continued on page 175)

1 Eyebrows

Sonia's eyebrows—which were slightly crooked—were a dominant feature on her face. So that's where I started for creating her softer look. **(a)** I trimmed Sonia's eyebrows with scissors and a razor comb so that the hairs would lay flatter on her face. This allowed me to see the shape of the brow. **(b)** I then began tweaking—two hairs here, one hair there—with tweezers. **(c)** Finally, I filled in a few places with a dark brown eyebrow pencil to balance out the shape.

2 Contouring and foundation

I used a yellow okra (think mustard) concealer on Sonia, since her skin tone is warm. I typically use yellow concealer on women with dark or Mediterranean skin tones: Indian, Brazilian, African American, Hispanic, Italian, or Greek. I also applied contouring foundation to help round out her face, creating a more oval-shaped face. **(a)** Using a concealer brush, I applied yellow okra highlighting concealer: ● Underneath the eyes ● At the sides of the nostrils ● From the forehead down the bridge of the nose ● On the centre of the chin ● On the sides of the mouth **(b)** Using a goat hair brush, I applied a contouring (dark) foundation: ● Underneath the cheekbones ● At the jaw line ● At the inner eye where the bridge of the nose meets the brow bone ● At the temples ● At the top of the forehead where the hairline meets the skin **(c)** Using a separate goat hair brush, I applied a very warm yellow foundation on top of the contouring and highlighting. I moved the brush in a soft, circular motion for optimal blending.

Tip Eyebrows are a prominent feature on the face so give them some love. I recommend using a razor instead of plucking with tweezers to make them lay flat. Eyebrows that lie flat appear smoother than those that don't. When using a razor comb, lift the eyebrow with the razor and turn in the opposite direction. Always put a comb underneath the razor to avoid taking away too much hair.

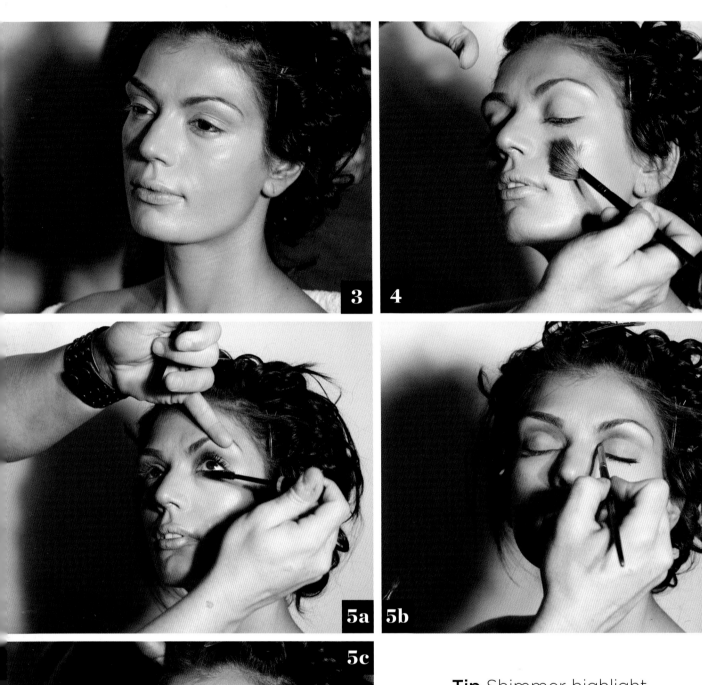

3

4

5a

5b

5c

Tip Shimmer highlight creates light and bone structure. You can "move" the cheekbone based on where you put your shimmer highlighter because shifting where the light reflects on the face gives the illusion of moving bones.

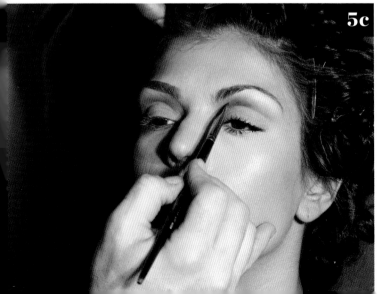

(continued from page 173)

3 Cheeks

Using a brush blush, I applied a peachy-pink cream blush on the apples of Sonia's cheeks. I moved the brush in small, circular strokes and thoroughly blended for a seamless look.

4 Highlighting

When highlighting Sonia's cheekbones I applied the Shimmer Highlight slightly higher than her natural cheekbone to draw the eye to a different point on her face. This trick gives the illusion of softening Sonia's square jaw.

5 Eyes

Sonia has wide-set eyes, which extend even further at the outer corner, so I wanted to balance the eyes with the rest of her features. **(a)** I put smoky-gray eye shadow in the crease of her eye and slightly above. I applied it darker at the centre of her eyelid, which was even with the outside corner of her mouth. **(b)** I added a light dusting of Empirical Gold eye shadow over the whole lid for a bit of subtle glamour without it looking too "Vegas showgirl." **(c)** Continuing to balance with black mascara, I applied the heaviest portion in the middle of her upper and lower lashes and less on the outside and inside corners of her eyes. **(d)** Instead of rimming the whole eye, I added a small bit of soft brown eyeliner only to the inner corners of her eyes. This helped give the eye some definition without looking overbearing or creating a heavy under-eye. **(e)** I completed the eyes with some false eyelashes. I decided to use individual lashes simply to fill in and compliment her real lashes. I avoided putting dark eyeliner around her eye, which is a more stereotypical look on an Indian woman. Remember, you want the focus to be on the eyes, not on the eye makeup.

6 Lips

Working with Sonia's normal colouring helped create full, natural-looking lips. **(a)** I applied a peachy-pink colour on Sonia's lips that matched the inside colour of her lips. **(b)** I finished off with a translucent shimmery pink gloss.

7 Setting the look

Using a powder brush, I set the makeup with a light dusting of translucent powder so as not to change the colour of the foundation and the blush.

SCOTT: How about diet?
SONIA: I eat whatever I want but in moderation. I stay away from all fried food.

SCOTT: How do you stay so disciplined?
SONIA: I just believe a lot. When you have faith, you can put your focus on trusting instead of worrying, and this allows you to be good to others. That's how I think a person becomes beautiful day by day. I also think it's about making conscious decisions. You have to believe that you are the most important person and everything you do to your body makes a difference.

Sonia's Reaction to Her Transformation

Scott really paid attention to my individual features and brought out the best of me, as opposed to a preconceived image of me. I never knew I should use a yellow concealer under my eyes, which blended better and enhanced my skin tone more. And the way he shaped my eyebrows... wow! My arch is so much cleaner, and they're finally even! I went right out and bought a razor comb."

The day after I met with Scott, I experimented with some of the tricks I learned from him and when I walked into work, I got so many compliments. Overall, I think my look is much smoother and fresher. I can't say enough of what a great experience it was for me."

Beauty of
whatever kind,
in its supreme
development,
invariably excites
the sensitive
soul to tears.
—Edgar Allan Poe

Sage:
Embracing the 1940s Glam Look

Sage knows how to turn a personal challenge into a tremendous opportunity. Having battled weight issues as a young girl, she now has a very healthy career as a plus-size model. On the board for Hearty Girls, Healthy Women, a non-profit organization based in Maine, USA, Sage is helping to raise awareness for the organization and advises young girls who are struggling with eating disorders and body image issues. As she puts it, "Just because you're larger doesn't mean you can't feel good about yourself and your body." It's this kind of self-respect that makes Sage all the more radiant.

In the course of our conversation, Sage told me she loved classic films of the 1930s and 1940s, Hollywood's Golden Age, which was something we had in common. She wistfully spoke of "that old Hollywood glamour" and wondered how it would feel to look like a star of that period. I decided to show her. The result was a 1940s glam look worthy of the red carpet—in any decade.

SCOTT: You began modeling when you were a teenager?

SAGE: That's right. I started modelling at fourteen, after I won a trip to Paris on the television talk show, "Good Day L.A." I ended up working as a model out of Los Angeles, and I had a lot of success in one year, but I couldn't keep my weight down. It's the classic story of a girl eating only 750 calories a day for a year, doing exactly what she was told...and it led to all sorts of health issues. So, I quit modelling, changed high schools, and eventually graduated from Sarah Lawrence College with a degree in comparative literature and theatre studies. Eventually I fell back into modelling, only this time for the plus-size division of an agency. I love plus-size modelling because it allows me to travel constantly. I'm also writing a book on body image to share my experience. I didn't know that what I was doing at fourteen was considered extreme dieting or anorexic behavior. And I really wish somebody

(continued on page 183)

Creating Sage's Look

1　**2**

Tip When you get flush, you're blushing from underneath. So you want to mimic this natural blush when putting on your makeup.

Tip When highlighting try to put the lighter colour where the sun might hit your face. Lightening these areas helps to draw the eye to these parts of your face.

(continued from page 181)

I wanted to give Sage the full effect of feeling like a 1940s Hollywood starlet, so I approached her transformation the same way they might have back then—right down to the pin curls.

Keep in mind that some of the makeup you see here is exaggerated for photography purposes. I'm not suggesting you use this much when putting it on yourself. Definitely go subtler for everyday purposes.

....

1 Contouring, concealer, and foundation

Sage's face was on the rounder side, so I wanted to added greater contrast to create more angles and definition in her face. **(a)** I used a goat hair brush and applied contouring (dark) foundation: • Underneath the jaw line • Underneath the cheekbones • Down the sides of the nose • On the tip of the nose • On the forehead **(b)** Using a concealer brush, I applied highlighting (light) concealer: • Under the eyes • Down the tip of the nose • In the middle of the forehead • At the centre of the chin **(c)** Using a separate goat hair brush, I applied a thin layer of pale beige cream foundation to counteract the redness in Sage's skin and give her a more cream-coloured complexion. *Remember: Effective application of contouring, highlighting, and foundation is about one thing: blending. I use brushes for application, which I believe provides the smoothest blend, but you can also use sponges or your fingers. Whatever you use, just be sure to blend, blend, blend. Oh, and did I mention you've got to blend?*

2 Cheeks

I applied a peachy-pink cream blush on the apples of Sage's cheeks. I applied the blush with a brush and kept blending in a circular motion to create a more natural-looking peaches-and-cream complexion. *Remember: To find the apples of your cheeks…simply smile.*

would've pulled me aside and said, "Look, you have an eating disorder." It would've saved me ten years of struggling with being really prejudiced against full-figured women. I had to work very hard to overcome my own bias against being a curvy woman. Now that I've embraced it, I feel really good in my own skin. It's ironic that the one thing I thought was holding me back is now the very thing that has made for such a wonderful life.

SCOTT: That's an important story about embracing who we are. So, how would you describe your eating habits now?
SAGE: I try to eat a balanced diet with lots of fruits and vegetables of different colours, because it really does reflect in your skin. I've always had issues with acne, so skin care's a real challenge. So, I take vitamins regularly to address it from the inside. I also use really natural skin-care products and use masks a couple of times a week.

SCOTT: What would you say you love most about yourself?
SAGE: I love my attitude. I haven't always had the same attitude, and I'm

(continued on page 185)

3 Lips

The distinguishing feature of the 1940s look is that of red hot lips. Sage already had nice full lips to pull this off, so a lot of reshaping wasn't necessary. **(a)** I lined Sage's lips with a Chinese red pencil, following her natural lip line. I then filled in her lip with the same red pencil to create a solid red lip. **(b)** I topped this off with a tinted amber glaze to give her lips a heavy shine.

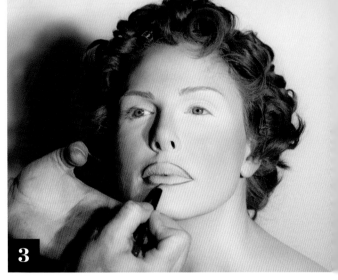

4 Eyebrows

Sage had clean, nicely shaped brows; I only needed to match them to her hair colour. Matching the brow colour to the hair colour is an important point for redheads; otherwise, you're simply a walking billboard that says, "Hey, I coloured my hair!"

For Sage, who has brown brows, I added mustard-colour eye shadow to her eyebrows with an angle brow brush. This had the effect of turning her brown brows into red brows since red hair is really brown hair with a lot of gold in it.

5 Eyes

Sage has fairly small eyelids, so I wanted to create a larger eyelid. **(a)** I put auburn eye shadow slightly above her normal crease. This trick helps to open up the eye and gives it a very feminine appearance. This colour matched her hair colour, so it would disappear into her skin and look as if she had no eye makeup on. **(b)** I blended the eye shadow into the inner corner of her eye and then faded it out toward the outside of the eye. **(c)** I also went underneath the eye with the same colour, which helped bring out her baby blues.

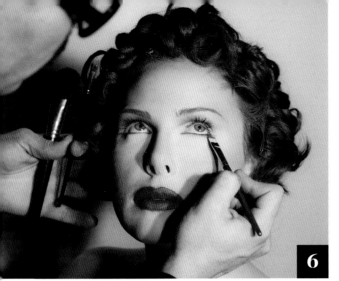

6

Eye-lashes

For Sage, I used individual false eyelashes only on the outer corners to elongate her eyes. I put no lashes on the inside of her eye, to help keep the inner eye area more open. I completed the eyes with lots and lots of mascara: always.

6

7

Setting the look

I finished off with a nice dusting of translucent powder so as not to change the colour of the foundation and the blush.

7

Tip Make sure you don't use a bright yellow because you don't want lemon brows!

Tip If you don't have a large eyelid, you can reshape the eye with colour. Simply placing your eye shadow just above the crease of your eye creates the illusion of a larger lid.

(continued from page 183)

grateful for the way I have come to see things. I feel really good about my body now. I work out four times a week and either go to the gym or do yoga classes. I try to remind myself that it's a luxury to be able to have time to work out because I know a lot of people who have children or work long hours who can't really find the time for it.

SCOTT: What are your biggest beauty challenges?
SAGE: Well, of course, I don't like the acne, as I mentioned. Something else I have trouble with is redness in the skin. Especially around the nose—that's a constant concern. I'd also like to look young forever! On the other hand, I want to age gracefully, so that's another challenge I look forward to embracing.

SCOTT: You mentioned you wanted to see what it felt like to walk down the red carpet in the 1940s. Why is that?
SAGE: That was Hollywood's Golden Age, and some of my favourite films are from that era. I just always loved the way they looked. It's a different kind of glamourous than we have today.

Sage's Reaction
to Her Transformation

'Scott took me to a whole other place I hadn't imagined existed.
I felt like a 1940s glamour puss. It's great that I now know how
to do this look, and I also feel like I can integrate the different
techniques into my normal routine. I mean, I love the way he did
my eyes and I could do this on a daily basis."

'I'm usually so insecure with the way I do my own makeup because
I have such difficulty covering blemishes and redness to the
point where I practically give up. I don't usually feel the level of

confidence that I did after Scott finished. It was a night-and-day difference. I also loved learning about what to do with my eyebrows as a redhead. I've always used a red eyebrow pencil and it made my eyebrows look brown. I've done that my whole life. But Scott showed me how to put yellow on my eyebrows instead."

"Overall the look was very showstopper, Scott definitely made me feel like a movie star!"

I would not suggest
women wear red lipstick
EVERY DAY.

Scott Barnes on Red Lipstick: Some Dos and Don'ts

Red lipstick is used to create a very specific look. I would not suggest women wear red lipstick every day. If red lipstick is your signature thing, you'd better have a whole style and wardrobe that go along with it. Gwen Stefani is a good example. She wears red lipstick well because she has an entire wardrobe and hairstyle that support it. You can't throw on sweats with red lipstick.

DON'T wear red lipstick: • When you're wearing red—Matching red with red is tricky. It's rarely the right shade, so it usually clashes. • When you're wearing bright green. Why would you want to look like a Christmas tree? • For funerals—For some reason, women like to do the "red lipstick with a black suit" thing when they're in mourning. I feel it reads too flirty, as in, "I can't wait to bury him...who's next!" • During the day in bright sunlight— It looks too harsh.

DO wear red lipstick: • In the evening • For black-tie events • With minimal makeup on the eye (or at least the allusion of minimal makeup on the eye), like Sage • If you're a redhead.

Judith Light ★

I just wanted to ENHANCE THE BEAUTY I saw when I looked at her.

Scott on Judith

Judith has an engaging magnetism, both on screen and off. While many of the characters she plays are brash, haughty types, in person she has enormous humility, gratitude, and great generosity of spirit. All these things make Judith incredibly sexy. And it's no wonder she has remained so beautiful, so remarkable, year after year.

In spite of our never having worked together before, Judith had immense trust in me as an artist. Her willingness to simply hand herself over to me revealed her own sense of confidence. It also demonstrated how well she understands the creative process. By not setting up a lot of parametres she left more room for inspiration. I didn't want to change Judith. I wasn't looking to make her into something else. I just wanted to enhance the beauty I saw when I looked at her.

Perhaps one of the things I admire most about Judith is her conviction to use her celebrity status in the service of others. She has become known as someone willing to speak out on tough issues: women's health, AIDS, and the gay and lesbian community. She spoke of her belief that "we, as human beings, all have a responsibility to be respectful of each other and our individual choices."It's this courage to take a stand that gives Judith enormous strength of character, and it resonates in every fiber of her being. It intensifies her beauty.

It's hard to define exactly why two people connect, and perhaps the why doesn't matter. The important point is that when a connection does happen, it's a rare and beautiful thing. Judith and I had an instant bond that made working together a true joy. And I knew she was somebody I wanted to have in my life for the rest of my life.

Judith on Beauty

It all began with a lip gloss. Not just any lip gloss—Scott Barnes' lip gloss. I had run out and I needed more. At the time, his makeup line had been temporarily discontinued, so getting my hands on this lip gloss was a near impossible task. It took tracking down Scott himself to obtain my much-needed cosmetic, and I received a shipment from the man himself. In the course of that transaction, I had a wonderful phone conversation with Scott, and that's when he told me about his book, *About Face*. He invited me to be a part of it, and I wholeheartedly accepted. After all, he had come through with my lip gloss.

On first meeting Scott, I felt an immediate familiarity with him that goes beyond words. It was a kind of connection that allowed me to trust him and say, "Look, you do whatever you want, whatever you see." And so he did. Scott saw me in an entirely new way, and he made me feel beautiful.

I'm in that age range where for several years now I've been asking myself, "Is it time to have plastic surgery?" It's a thought that concerns me, not because I don't understand it or am opposed to it. I'm not one of these people who wonder "Why do women do that?" I totally get why women do that! And there are days when I, too, am steps away from picking up the phone and making that appointment. I believe I would look better to myself. But then I step back and ask whether or not I am simply buying into a cultural concept that youthfulness is better. Do I really need this?

It's a conflict that I and many other women struggle with.

As women, as human beings, I think we do ourselves a tremendous disservice. We think we see ourselves clearly. But the vision of ourselves is blurred by the messages we receive from our culture, our media, and by the programming of our own thoughts, which is based on how we were brought up. All these filters through which we perceive ourselves only cloud our ability to see our real self. So, are we able to see our real beauty, the beauty that comes with age—the beauty of tremendous wisdom and power and generosity?

Years ago I went to a yoga camp in New Mexico, USA. I remember one class where the instructor brought in these photographs and she said, "Pick the photograph that most represents either who you are or who you want to be." I thought for sure I would pick the photo of a woman who was young and beautiful. But I kept finding myself drawn to this one photograph of an old, wrinkled Indian woman. She was wrapped in a beautiful embroidered shawl and sitting in front of some mountains. I finally realized that I was attracted to her soul. In her face was knowledge and ownership of self. I was completely stunned by my

I try to listen from within and learn to SURRENDER.

response to that photograph. It told me that's who I long to be, a woman of substance—a woman who values experience and spirituality over the more superficial things I'm told by my society to value.

There's a kind of tenderness that we don't afford each other often enough. We need to support each other more as we go through this process called life so that we don't feel like we're struggling alone. I'm not talking about "women banding together." I'm talking about an empathetic connection as human beings. So often, we go through our busy lives encountering other individuals who make us impatient and we don't stop long enough to really take in the person whose holding up the line because, as they're digging through their change purse, their fingers don't operate as quickly as they once did or they've got something more pressing on their mind. We don't afford each other that kind of compassion,

tolerance, or generosity of spirit. I think it was Abraham Lincoln who suggested we operate as "the better angels of our nature," which goes to the question of "What is it that makes us beautiful?"

It's certainly another source of beauty, doing things that make us feel beautiful. Because in the doing, we are nurturing our soul, and that's a beauty that goes beyond the physical to the real self. But if you're only listening to all the external messages, we can never become the beauty we are meant to be.

We've got to focus on the things that enlighten us, empower us, and that make us feel good about ourselves. So, I work at this. I do yoga. I walk. I eat as well as I can. I meditate. I focus on the spiritual side of my nature. I work on gratitude. I try to listen from within and learn to surrender. Fortunately, I also have a husband who thinks I am beautiful, no matter what age I am. I'm incredibly

blessed with that. And I have close friends who tell me I look terrific. It's important to listen to those people around you who really love you and who have your best interests at heart, especially when your own mind is telling you something different. And I worry less when I come across people like Scott Barnes because I know Scott will make me look as beautiful as I can feel inside. It provides a feeling of great relief, and it helps quiet those thoughts of "Oh, my neck" or "Oh, my jowls." When you look at the photograph of me, you won't see any of that. That's because Scott's an artist, a real artist, much like the old Italian masters, in the way he can make a woman look and feel beautiful.

And he makes phenomenal lip gloss.

Carmelita:
Experimenting with Colour for More Drama

Carmelita is a Brazilian beauty. She's originally from Sao Paolo, where the rest of her family still resides. She currently models, but having recently completed a degree in biology, she's working toward becoming a veterinarian. Her love for animals is evident as her face lights up when she's talking about her boxer and two pinchers. Unfortunately, she had to leave them behind in Brazil.

Carmelita's angular face gives her a feline quality I wanted to capitalize on. I knew I needed to balance out her long jaw and reshape her hairline for a cleaner, more balanced look. Also, as beautiful as Carmelita looks naturally, I wanted to show her that she could unleash her diva within!

Scott + Carmelita Talk ...

SCOTT: Do you ever get mistaken for being African American?
CARMELITA: Yes, and I always correct these people. Brazilian women are a mixture of races, even though they have the skin colour and strong features that look similar to those of African-American women.

SCOTT: Do you have any favourite foods or drinks?
CARMELITA: A Brazilian dish: beans, rice, and meat. I like African food also and Italian. I'm not a vegetarian; I like my meat. I stay away from French fries. I eat no fried foods in general. And I drink wine, juice, tea... everything.

SCOTT: Do you like to exercise?
CARMELITA: I like to ride the bicycle at the gym, for my legs. I go to the gym, but not every day since I don't always have the time. But I walk every morning for about thirty minutes.

SCOTT: Do you like to wear makeup?
CARMELITA: Yes, but I like to wear very natural

(continued on page 197)

Creating, Carmelita's Look

Carmelita was used to going with a natural, no-makeup look. I wanted to show her that she had room to experiment with much more colour since she has so much depth to her dark skin. My goal was to create a dazzling presence that would rival any dance-floor diva.

2a **2b**

1 Prepping the face

Sometimes, like in Carmelita's case, you'll want to address unwanted facial hair or an uneven hairline before beginning makeup application to achieve a cleaner, more polished look. This helps bring the focus into the centre of the face, to your eyes, nose, and mouth. • Hairline and upper lip: Using a razor comb I trimmed Carmelita's hairline to take the jagged edges off and soften the frame of her face. I also removed the fuzz from her upper lip. • Eyebrows: Using a razor comb, I thinned and shaped Carmelita's eyebrows and then plucked a few stragglers with tweezers. *Remember: When shaping the eyebrows, always strive for minimal plucking with tweezers to avoid permanently damaging the hair follicles.*

2 Contouring, highlighting, and foundation

Carmelita's got terrific facial bones which make for great angles. So, when applying foundation, I wanted to be sure I didn't flatten out her face by using only one colour of foundation. Carmelita's skin tone contains both red and yellow pigment. This combination of colours is why Carmelita has a bronzy colour to her skin. Instead of trying to match one colour or the other, I used both to stay as close as possible to the light and dark of her natural colouring. **(a)** Using light strokes with a goat hair brush, I applied a reddish-burgundy contouring foundation: • At the bottom of the chin, instead of underneath the jaw line (to give the illusion of shortening the chin) • Underneath the cheekbones • On the sides of the nose • At the inner eye where the bridge of the nose meets the brow bone • At the temples • Under the tip of the nose (This gives the illusion of shortening the nose.) • At the top of the forehead where the hairline meets the skin **(b)** Using a concealer brush, I applied yellow highlighting concealer: • On top of the cheekbones • Underneath the eyes • From the forehead down the bridge of the nose • On the upper part of the chin (This gives the illusion of shortening the chin since the eye is drawn to where the light hits the chin.) **(c)** Using a separate goat hair brush, I applied a thin layer of bronze cream foundation on top of the contouring and highlighting. *Remember: Blend thoroughly, moving the brush in a circular motion to marry all the colours and achieve the smoothest finish. Remember: If you have dark skin, you should have two or three foundations that you can blend to create a more natural-looking foundation with greater dimension. Dark skin is never one colour. When applying foundation you want to attempt to mimic the natural colour of these different skin tones; otherwise, you risk flattening out your face by making it either too light or too dark.*

(continued from page 195)

makeup, all organic; and not too much makeup.
I like to look very natural. If I'm going out, I will put on mascara and blush and some gloss. But I find it's very difficult to buy the right blushes and shadows for my skin colour, so I usually go without.

SCOTT: What do you do for skin care?
CARMELITA: For cleaning my face, I use a soft cleanser in the morning and then I put on lotion. I don't put too much on my skin because I prefer my skin to be very natural. At night, I always wash my face and put on cream too.

SCOTT: Are there things about yourself that you like or dislike?
CARMELITA: I don't like my hair, because it is so short. So, I put extensions in my hair to make it longer. You can see I have extensions in now! I think I like nearly everything else about myself. If I could change one thing, I would maybe change my butt, because it is so skinny.

(continued on page 199)

I gently pressed the powder puff over her face to **SET THE MAKEUP.**

3

4

5a

5b

3 Cheeks

I applied a reddish-burgundy cream blush to the apples of Carmelita's cheeks and blended in circular strokes for a seamless transition.

4 Setting the look

As I've mentioned before, this is a very important step for creating a flawless finish. You can use either a loose powder with colour or a translucent powder. I opted to use a light tan loose powder with a yellow under-tone. This helped to bring out the bronze tone in Carmelita's skin. **(a)** With a very large fluffy powder brush, I loosely dusted powder all over Carmelita's face and neck. **(b)** I tapped the excess powder from the brush onto a powder puff. I then folded the puff as though I were making a taco and smushed the powder into the puff. This trick buries the excess powder into the puff so that it doesn't end up on your face. **(c)** I gently pressed the powder puff over her face to set the makeup.

5 Lips

To select the lip liner colour, I used the darkest spot of Carmelita's lip, which turned out to be close to a chocolate-burgundy colour. **(a)** I lined Carmelita's lips follow-ing her lip line. **(b)** I shaded the inside inner corners of her lips to create more depth on the inside of her lips. **(c)** I later finished the lips off with lip gloss (see step 7 on page 201).

(continued from page 197)

SCOTT: Who do you consider beautiful?
CARMELITA: Beyoncé.

SCOTT: Is it difficult to be such a beautiful woman?
CARMELITA: I don't consider myself to be a pretty lady. It's only when I have makeup put on me that I think I can look pretty. Makeup can change the face so much, so if you have beautiful makeup, then you can become beautiful!

Using separate brushes
is the best way to
AVOID MIXING eye shadow
colours in their cases as well.

6a 6b

6 Eyes

I mentioned earlier that Carmelita has red and yellow undertones. I used the same reddish-burgundy that I used for contouring as an eye shadow base, creating depth and contour around her eyes. I used different eye shadow brushes for each of the following steps for cleaner application. Using separate brushes is the best way to avoid mixing eye shadow colours in their cases as well. **(a)** First I hollowed out her eye by blending the reddish-burgundy contouring powder in the crease of her eye and in the inner corner of her brow bone. **(b)** I layered a purple eye shadow right in the crease and just above it. **(c)** I added a fine line of black eye shadow using a very thin eyeliner brush in the crease for a more dramatic effect. (We're talking diva here!) **(d)** I applied the reddish-burgundy contouring shadow underneath the eye as well, using a brush with a very fine, slightly chiseled point. **(e)** I lined the eye with a black pencil to give the eye some depth, and I outlined from the middle of the lower eyelid to the middle of the top eyelid to draw the focus to her outer eye, which gave the effect of opening up her eyes. (Applying the liner towards the inside of her eyes would have the effect of "closing" her eyes slightly, making them appear smaller and closer together.) **(f)** Since we were going for high drama with Carmelita, I finished off with purple glitter on her eyelids. Just be sure not to "drip" glitter all over other areas of your face; otherwise, you'll be noticed for all that glitter on your face, not your own beauty. **(g)** I finally added some upper and lower false eyelashes for the full diva effect. *Warning: Caucasians, don't try this at home! If you apply these colours on your fair skin, it will end up looking like you were in a scary accident!*

7 Lip gloss

I finished the lips with a Black Cherry Patent Leather lip gloss.

Carmelita's Reaction
to Her Transformation

"I look so different! I love the makeup so much—the colour of my skin, the colour on my eyes, the way he made my face look not so long and skinny—everything's so, so pretty. Scott used different colours for the base of my skin. My skin colour is very dark in some parts, but not in all parts. So, I've learned how to use different colours for this base instead of using just one colour. This pleases me very much.

I also know now that using more colour for my face, like purples or reds, is very good for me. Scott put it on my eyes, a little bit on my lips, and on my nails. Normally, I would wear black or darker colours. Now that seems boring. He also used more colour in my cheeks, like red, and put black eyeliner inside my eye. It makes such a big difference to use brighter colours. This makes me feel very chic."

Linda:
Time-Saving Tips for the Busy Woman

Linda has had a big year: she got married, bought a house, and became pregnant. Weekdays, she works full time for an Italian designer in New York City. On weekends, she is fixing up the new house, and basically trying to get as much done as possible before the baby arrives. Linda doesn't slow down long enough to look in the mirror, much less devote time to a beauty regimen. Linda used to "love to play with makeup" when her life was less complicated, "but now," she told me, "I've completely let myself go."

I see too many women fall into this trap. They're juggling so many things, and they make less time for themselves. Unfortunately, they also start to feel less good about themselves, and often, their self-worth and their relationships suffer. Linda admitted she was feeling less beautiful over the past year, especially since she had gotten pregnant. My hope was that Linda's transformation would help her reconnect to her womanliness and give her a more positive self-image. As Linda transformed, it was thrilling to watch her regain a sense of her own sex appeal.

SCOTT: Is it safe to assume that given your very busy life, you have a pretty simple skin-care routine?
LINDA: Yes, it's very basic. Most mornings I wash and then moisturize. I usually buy the chemist's brands, nothing expensive. I buy different brands, but the one brand I have been using since I was a kid is Nivea. I use their oldest facial cream, which is this really heavy, thick cream that feels almost like cold cream. It's a classic, and I use it morning, day, evening, all the time.

SCOTT: Do you ever take time out for yourself?
LINDA: Not really. I certainly don't pamper myself anymore—I rarely go get a manicure, I don't do my makeup...I feel like I've completely let myself go. I have just been overwhelmed with everything going on. I work full-time, then I got married, we bought the house, and we got pregnant...everything happened in a year. And I haven't really had time off to myself at all. It'd be nice to feel like a woman again.

(continued on page 207)

Creating Linda's Look

1a

1b

1c

Time-Saving Tip

You can always spot-conceal by putting concealer only in those places where it is really needed: under the eyes, around the sides of the nostrils, and over any blemishes. Just make sure you blend these places really well. Adding a quick dusting of translucent powder on top will help with this.

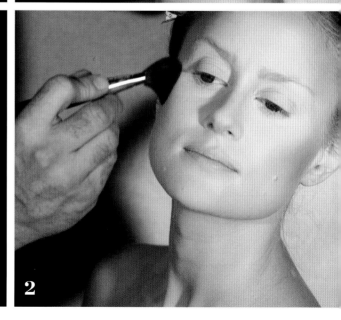

2

Just because you get married doesn't mean it's over. Just because you're having a baby doesn't mean it's over. Actually, it's just the beginning. Your priorities may shift, but you don't want to forget about taking care of yourself. Remember, half of feeling good is looking good, and looking good leads to feeling good. Putting on makeup doesn't have to be a time-consuming process. But it's worth the few minutes it takes to make yourself feel better. Here are the steps for creating Linda's look, as well as some time-saving tips.

1 Contouring, highlighting, and foundation

I did very light contouring for Linda since her colouring is so fair. **(a)** With extremely light strokes, I applied contouring (dark) foundation: • Underneath the cheekbones • On top of the forehead • At the temples **(b)** Using a concealer brush, I applied highlighting (light) concealer: • Under the eyes • Down the tip of the nose • In the middle of the forehead • At the centre of the chin **(c)** Using a separate goat hair brush, I applied a thin layer of cream beige foundation, which I thoroughly blended with the contouring and highlighting for a smooth finish.

2 Cheeks

Linda's face is on the longer side, so I wanted to help shorten it some by making sure I put the blush on the apples of her cheeks. Placing the blush underneath her cheekbones would have had the effect of making her face look longer and more drawn out.

Moving the brush in a circular motion, I applied a pale-pink cream blush on the apples of her cheeks, a colour that was a warmer rather than cooler pink. This colour complimented her fair features with just a hint of colour without being too dramatic.

(continued from page 205)

SCOTT: What do you love best about being a woman?
LINDA: I love to wear dresses. I'm a girly girl... I rarely wear jeans.

SCOTT: Where are you from originally?
LINDA: Finland. But I've been living In the United States for more than fifteen years.

SCOTT: Do you see a difference in the way women approach beauty in Finland versus here in the States?
LINDA: Yes, Finnish women don't put as much time into their appearance as American women...for better or worse. It seems like women here spend much more time taking care of themselves, focusing on things like teeth whitening.

SCOTT: What is your idea of beautiful?
LINDA: My nanny, who is now a dear friend of mine, used to say, "Many a cake is pretty on the outside..." meaning that even if the frosting looks great, it doesn't mean the cake will actually taste good. So, I learned very early that being beautiful isn't about a person's exterior. True beauty is all about how you treat other people; being beautiful is about being nice to everyone around you.

3a

3b

4a

4b

4c

Time-Saving Tip

If you've got no time to think about lip liner and colour, simply go with a tinted lip gloss. A little gloss can go a long way toward giving you a fresh, healthy appearance. Never leave home without your gloss.

3 Lips

Linda has nice full lips, so it was really a matter of bringing out what she's already got and using colours that would compliment her sparkling blue eyes with a tiny bit of colour. No reshaping of the lips was necessary. **(a)** I lined Linda's lips with a taupe lip liner, a colour that was one shade darker than her lip colour, by following her natural lip border. **(b)** I filled in with a pastel pink lipstick. **(c)** I completed with a sheer lip gloss.

4 Eyes

Linda's eyes are close-set, so I kept everything heavier on the outside corners of her eyes to give the illusion that her eyes are a little farther apart. **(a)** I covered the whole eye with cream beige foundation—the same that I used earlier on her face. This gave me a more even base on which to layer colour since Linda' eyelids had touches of red pigment in them. **(b)** I applied a smoky gray eye shadow on the top lid along the outside half of the lash line. **(c)** Using this same smoky gray shadow, I filled in at the crease of the eye and on the outside half of the upper lid. **(d)** I lined the whole inside of the eye—upper and lower—with a black Maybelline pencil to really accentuate her blue eyes. **(e)** I went back in with the smoky gray eye shadow and applied a thin line of colour underneath the eye. I delicately smudged the line after applying for a softer effect. I used this colour to create a more sultry, smoky look for Linda. **(f)** I finished off with black mascara on both the upper and lower lashes, with an emphasis on the outside corners of her lashes to draw the eyes outward.

5 Setting the Look

Using a fan brush, I softly dusted champagne shimmer highlight on the tops of her cheekbones, forehead, and nose to add a warm overall glow to the look and followed that with a light dusting of translucent powder.

Time-Saving Tip

Eyeliner can do a lot in terms of quickly enhancing your eyes if you don't have a lot of time. The same is true with mascara. You can line the inside rim of the eye—both the upper and lower lids—and use either black or brown liner. Just be careful that you don't make it too harsh-looking, if you have time to apply only minimal makeup.

Time-Saving Tip

Simply put a tiny bit of shadow along the crease of your eye using your fingers, just to give your eyes some dimension.

REACTIONS...

Linda's Reaction to Her Transformation

"I have to say, I've never felt so glamourous in my whole life. I feel ten years younger! Also my husband looked at me in a fresh way again, and that was definitely nice. I didn't want to wash it off! So, now I've started to take a little extra time in the morning. And when I do something as simple as put mascara and liner on my eye, it makes a

big difference. Just putting in that extra five minutes...and I actually had to wake up five minutes earlier just to do that one little thing...but it makes all the difference! It's true that you really do feel better about yourself if you feel like you look good. I can even feel a difference in the way that I work; I work with more confidence. I feel

100 percent more confident with makeup on. I feel like a woman again and that's really nice. So, I think a woman should really try and make the effort. And now, if my husband and I go out somewhere, I wear a bit more makeup. A little bit goes a long way. I do it for my husband. But I also do it for myself."

"I want to say one more thing. Scott's whole 'glow' thing has always fascinated me, and it was incredible to see up close the way he applies the highlights and the lowlights. At one point he put a little bit of sheen on the tip of my nose—a shimmery highlight—and it transformed my face in a really surprising way."

Danielle:
Shifting from Conservative to High-Impact

It would be easy to label Danielle as conservative. She graduated with a finance degree from Cornell University and now works for Bank of America. She's married and has two dogs (a miniature pinscher and a Brussels griffin) and does "adult things" on the weekends with her husband. But I only had to scratch the surface to discover that Danielle is anything but conventional. She has traveled to numerous countries, she's a serious hiker, and she climbs mountains—quite literally, having already scaled Mount Kilimanjaro. In addition to working long hours, she stays active playing tennis, going biking, or rollerblading. Next year, she plans to run the Chicago Marathon, simply because "it helps me to have a goal for physical fitness."

Danielle's a smart, fast-moving woman, and there's nothing stuffy or cautious about her—except her appearance. Her moderate, tailored look doesn't match her adventurous, goal-driven personality. It was time to update her look. Always open to something new and different, Danielle courageously took the plunge. Danielle's new look had such dramatic impact that even her husband barely recognized her.

Scott + Danielle Talk ...

SCOTT: What is your typical beauty routine?
DANIELLE: I'm pretty basic. I don't really have a beauty routine. I usually get up late and roll out to work in about twenty minutes. So, that time consists of taking a shower, washing my face, putting on moisturizer with some protection, powder, mascara, and that's it. Oh, and usually some Chapstick. Today I actually put on some blush because I was concerned about my "before" shot. But in general, I'd say that I don't like to spend a lot of time focusing on me.

SCOTT: How about at night?
DANIELLE: I usually take a shower, wash my face, and then use a different moisturizer, a heavy night cream. No eye cream yet, although I'm told I'm supposed to start doing that. They say you're supposed to do it before you need it.

SCOTT: Are there things about yourself you wish you could change?

(continued on page 215)

Creating Danielle's Look

1a

1b

3

Tip Squint when looking at Danielle's contouring photo to better see the dark and light areas on her face.

Tip Be careful not to overdo the lining in the centre of the bottom lip; otherwise, you'll make the lower lip look too small. You still want the lips to look as full and voluptuous as possible, but balanced.

(continued from page 213)

Daniel has a lovely oval face with pretty eyes and a beautiful nose and mouth. But she's faced with the same challenges many Asian women deal with: small eyes and no cheekbones. The trick to accentuating these features is to contour the face and elongate the eyes.

....

1 Contouring, highlighting, and foundation

Most Asian faces are flatter planes. So, with Danielle, I needed to create sharper angles and "pop out the bones" with contouring and highlighting. *Remember: Keep in mind this rule of thumb when contouring and highlighting: Light adds, and dark takes away.* **(a)** Using light strokes with a goat hair brush, I applied contouring (dark) foundation: • Underneath the jaw line • Underneath the cheekbones • On the sides of the nose • At the inner eye where the bridge of the nose meets the brow bone • At the temples • Under the tip of the nose (gives the illusion of shortening the nose) **(b)** With shorter brushstrokes, I used a concealer brush to apply highlighting (light) concealer: • On top of the cheekbones • Underneath the eyebrows • On the bridge of the nose • At the centre of the chin *Remember: When highlighting, try to put the lighter colour where the sun might hit your face. Lightening these areas helps to draw the eye to these parts of your face.* **(c)** Using a separate goat hair brush, I applied a thin layer of warm beige cream foundation, moving the brush in small circles to delicately blend on top of the contouring and highlighting.

2 Cheeks

I used peachy-pink cream blush for Danielle's cheeks. This colour, added some vibrancy to her cheeks. **(a)** I put a dab of cream blush on my finger and applied it to the apples of her cheeks. **(b)** I then used the foundation brush to blend it in, moving in a circular motion for a seamless transition between foundation and blush.

3 Lips

Danielle has a nice full lower lip. But it seemed to overpower her top lip, so I wanted to balance lower with upper. I used more muted colours so that the primary focus would remain on her eyes. **(a)** I followed the border of Danielle's upper lip with a dusty rose pencil. **(b)** I applied this same lip colour to the inside centre of her lower lip. This trick creates the illusion that the mouth is open, even when it's closed—pretty sexy, right? It also helps minimize the bottom lip, so it looks more balanced. **(c)** I finished off with a fleshy-coloured sheer gloss.

DANIELLE: Probably if there was something I wish I could change about my look, I'd rather have glowing skin. I don't have great skin, by any means. It's something I've never had, so yeah, I'd love to have great, flawless, glowing skin. Something I feel has always made me different is my eyes. And my lips—I have fuller lips. So, these are things I've grown to appreciate about my face.

SCOTT: Do you have a certain idea of what "beautiful" is to you?
DANIELLE: I think beauty is something timeless, natural. I believe there's something attractive in everyone. I think it's about finding a way to highlight whatever that something is. So, perhaps beautiful is about finding your uniqueness.

4a

4b

4c

5a

5b

Tip When filling in eyebrows, always follow your brow bone. And if you extend your eyeliner on your eye, be sure to also extend the eyebrow tail the same length so the brow doesn't stop short.

4 Eyes

To give the illusion of a larger eye, I elongated the length of the Danielle's eyes in both directions to give her eyes more magnetism. **(a)** With a black eyeliner pencil, I lined her whole eye, making sure to extend the inner corner and outer corner of the eye. **(b)** With a medium eye shadow brush, I applied a black eye shadow and kept blending it out to create more width and depth. In general, the more you blend, the softer the effect. **(c)** I finished off with a demi lash on the outside corner of her eye. Demi lashes are better than full lashes for Asian eyes, because if you put eyelashes in the inner corners, it has a tendency to make the eyes look too close together.

5 Eyebrows

Asian eyebrows have a tendency to grow straight out, so it sometimes looks like the eyebrows are unruly. Danielle has well-shaped eyebrows naturally, so it was more about filling them in and getting them to lie flat than about reshaping them. **(a)** I did some minimal trimming with the razor comb and plucked a stray hair or two to flatten the brows. **(b)** I filled in the brow with a light brown eyebrow pencil. The wax from the pencil helps smooth down the hairs. Also, the darker hairs in the brow already create enough depth, so filling in with a lighter colour still results in a dark eyebrow without the eyebrow appearing too overdrawn, as it would with a darker eyebrow pencil colour.

Tip To create a demi lash, simply cut a regular pair of false eyelashes in half. Then be sure to use the outside half of the lash for the outside corner of the eye. You can also double up these two halves and place one on top of the other for one thick demi lash for added drama.

Danielle's Reaction
to Her Transformation

'Scott did things I never would've done to myself because I never would've even known to try them. Like the dramatic eye colours. I think maybe one of the reasons why my daily look is so plain is because I've never experimented with my eyes. I also had no idea that the contouring of the cheeks could have such a dramatic result. I would definitely do this for an evening event when I want more impact. I had been considering changing the shape of my eyebrows—going to an eyebrow specialist—because they can change your face. But Scott didn't really do anything to them

beyond minimal trimming and applying makeup, yet suddenly I
really love the way they look. They really seem to fit my face just
from the subtle changes in makeup."

"The experience has definitely given me a different sense of
confidence. It's almost surreal to see how I was before. I feel like
my regular look is no longer adequate. It's like I'm a totally different person. I think this is the most beautiful I've ever been in my
entire life!"

Lauren:
Blending Cooler Tones for More Sizzle and Pop

Here's my twist on a classic American beauty. Born in Champagne, Illinois, USA, Lauren has a sunny look and demeanor that make her the perfect model for clients who want the wholesome, girl-next-door or bride-to-be type. While not dissatisfied with her look (she works all the time), Lauren expressed interest in taking a new direction. Without drastically changing her look, I wanted to unearth a more timeless beauty, more reminiscent of a Catherine Deneuve. With her transformation, we took Lauren from Champagne, Illinois, to Champagne, France, the birthplace of sparkling white wine.

Scott + Lauren Talk …

SCOTT: In the morning when you get up, what do you do?

LAUREN: I wash my face and I put on a tinted sunscreen with an SPF of 15 or 30. That's pretty much it for the morning. If I have to put on makeup, I use some tinted moisturizer, concealer, sometimes mascara, and blush.

SCOTT: How about at the end of the day?

LAUREN: At night I'm stricter. I always cleanse, and use toner and moisturizer; I put a lot of moisturizer on my eyes. I also try to drink a lot of water before I go to bed. I try to drink two liters a day. I notice a difference in my skin with travelling on planes all the time. The water helps a lot.

(continued on page 223)

Creating, Lauren's Look

1a

1b

1c

1d

With Lauren, I wanted to shift the focus from her smile to her eyes, which tended to get lost. Lauren has hooded eyes, and it can be challenging to make hooded eyes appear more open. With her fair colouring, I knew I couldn't put a lot of additional colour on her face. I also knew that shifting her colouring from warmer tones to cooler, icy tones would help accentuate her piercing blue eyes.

1 Contouring, highlighting, and foundation

I cooled down Lauren's skin using a foundation that didn't have a lot of yellow tone in it, which tends to give a warmer look. Instead, I used a very cool neutral (a beige-pink tone). A cooler, "icier" foundation with blue in it allowed the skin to reflect back into the cool blue of her eyes for more depth. And when I say "blue," I mean a very subtle undertone; we weren't trying to create a Smurfette! **(a)** Using light strokes with a goat hair brush, I applied contouring (dark) foundation: • Underneath the jaw line • Underneath the cheekbones **(b)** With short brush strokes, I used a concealer brush to apply highlighting (light) concealer: • Under the eyes • On top of the cheekbones • Underneath the eyebrows • On the bridge of the nose • At the centre of the chin **(c)** Using a separate goat hair brush, I applied a thin layer of cooler beige-pink cream foundation on top of the contouring and highlighting and blended thoroughly, marrying all the colours together for a seamless transition between colours.

(continued from page 221)

SCOTT: What would you say is the most important thing for staying beautiful?
LAUREN: Exercise. I always exercise. For a while it was cardio and weight training, but now I'm doing more cardio and Pilates. I do a class here in New York that's all isometrics at a ballet bar—it's Pilates that incorporates natural body movements. All lengthening and strengthening, that's my favourite.

SCOTT: Are there models you admire?
LAUREN: Yes, Cindy Crawford and Heidi Klum. I think they're two women who have set great examples for what modelling can be. They've got great careers, and they balance them with an incredibly strong family life, which is really important to me. They also have maintained really wholesome images, which I admire. So, they've found a way to have the whole package.

(continued on page 225)

Remember, half of feeling good
is looking good,
and looking good leads
to FEELING GOOD.

3a **3b**

Tip Make sure to keep the highlighter on the apples of your cheeks; otherwise, your skin will look greasy. It's called a highlighter for a reason. Use it to hit the high points on your face.

(continued from page 223)

SCOTT: Do you think women spend too much time on their appearance?
LAUREN: In one sense, it's so great to be able to express yourself physically and have fun with makeup and show how great you can look. But I do think sometimes that women might take it a little too far. They don't fully appreciate the way they are, and they all start trying to look the same. I really believe that each of us is special. I think it'd be nice if everyone could embrace what they have and play with what they have. For example, I've always wanted to be really, really tan, but I'm not. I'm Swedish and I'm light, so I embrace that.

SCOTT: Is there something about yourself that you're most proud of?
LAUREN: I like my skin, probably because I've taken good care of it. Growing up in Florida, USA, I was always out in the sun. And my dad, a doctor, would always say, "Sunscreen, sunscreen, sunscreen," when my girlfriends were going to tanning spas and lying out. So, I was pretty strict with myself.

(continued on page 227)

2 Eyes

Lauren has a dark blue ring around the outside of her iris, which was hard to see. While the cooler foundation helped to wake up the blue in Lauren's eyes, I knew we could open them up even more. But I also knew I would have to use minimal eye shadow, since Lauren has a hooded eye. Heavy colour would only result in minimizing her eyes. What little colour I did use was a very, very pale gray, a colour I call Cashmere, which provides very soft, subtle shading. **(a)** I asked Lauren to keep her eye open and look straight ahead. Using a soft brush, I placed the Cashmere eye shadow directly above where the eye was open. This creates a colour wash and provides a bit of depth without adding a lot of colour. Think: creating a "shadow" in the eye. **(b)** I curled her eyelashes with an eyelash curler. **(c)** I applied a thin coat of black mascara. **(d)** I applied individual false eyelashes. I used three different lengths of lashes to create a kind of starburst effect. This helps keep the eye airy and open. A heavy lash would have the effect of closing up the eye. *Remember: Placement of individual false eyelashes is key. Putting the lashes on the outside corner keeps the eye more open and pulls the eye out from the centre of the face. Putting the lashes on the inside of the eye, on the other hand, gives a more doe-eyed appearance.*

3 Cheeks

Instead of using a blush, I used a champagne shimmer highlighter on the apples of Lauren's cheeks. I didn't want to introduce pink into the skin because I wanted the skin to remain a cool tone.

Cooler, icey tones would help accentuate her piercing blue eyes.

4a

4b

4c

Tip Brushing dry lips also gets the blood flowing, which makes your lips look fuller with more colour!

4 Lips

Before applying any lip colour, I showed Lauren how she could smooth out dry, chapped lips by using a lip balm and a boar's hair brush. (You can find a natural bristle brush at your local health food store. A plastic toothbrush is too abrasive on your lips.) I scrubbed the lips back and forth to gently exfoliate and slough off the dead skin. I wanted to balance Lauren's upper lip with her bottom lip since she has a thinner upper lip. But I didn't want to minimize the bottom lip, as I did with Danielle. I wanted to enhance her top lip. So, I filled out her top lip with a trick I call "connecting the twin peaks." **(1)** With a lip liner that matched her natural lip colour, I lightly connected the two highest points ("twin peaks") on Lauren's upper lip to give the illusion of more fullness. **(2)** I filled in the rest of the lip with a beige full-coverage lip gloss to complete the look.

5 Setting the look

I finished off with a nice dusting of translucent powder so as not to change the colour of the foundation and the blush.

Tip To create more fullness in the top lip without overlining, lightly connect over the peaks with a natural-coloured lip liner. This gives the illusion of a more pouty lip and is a nice update to the old "cupid bow" lips.

(continued from page 225)

SCOTT: What are you least proud of?
LAUREN: Well, one thing I don't like about myself is that I have to work out so hard, so often. Food is my biggest battle. I love food, but it conflicts with my career. I try to eat a lot of fruits and vegetables and protein, but I still eat the things I want to eat, including things that are not good for me, like margaritas and quesos. That means I have to work out a lot—every day, for one to two hours.

Lauren's Reaction
to Her Transformation

"My skin looked like porcelain! I've always had the clean, fresh look for shoots like bridal stories, but nothing like what Scott did with the grays and cooler colours. I've always tried to enhance my eyes, bring out the blue, and always try to make my skin look dewy and fresh, but I've never tried using anything but warm colours. It's amazing the difference a cooler shade can make."

"The other thing was the eyelashes...I really want to get good with false eyelashes because they really opened up my eyes and added a kind of sparkle. The other great trick I now use is drawing the line on top, straight across, on my upper lip. It definitely makes my lips look fuller."

"I'm excited to have learned how to create a new look. It's so easy to get stuck in what I find comfortable and what I know looks okay. So I don't experiment. It was really nice to learn how to do something so glamourous for a change."

Kim Kardashian ★

Scott on Kim

Kim and I had never met before her transformation, but I knew she was a very pretty woman. I soon discovered upon meeting Kim that she is also very intelligent. She has an entrepreneurial spirit and seems to know how to turn any situation to her advantage—in a way that shows she inherently understands the awesome power and necessity of marketing in the world of showbiz, which is amazing considering she's still so young and relatively new to the business. We saw her in action when she intentionally left our studio sporting a blonde wig without letting on that it was just that—a wig. She knew going from brunette to blonde would work the paparazzi into a lather. And sure enough, she had the talk shows and the tabloids buzzing about her "new look." Kim waited two days before finally revealing that she was wearing a wig, which of course created another flurry of excitement. Like I said, she intrinsically gets it.

If that isn't impressive enough, Kim is also hard-working. She starts her day at 5:00 a.m. so that she can get in a workout before moving on to manage her various businesses. And the best part? With all she has going on, Kim still maintains a positive and energetic spirit. She has this amazing way of lighting up a room that makes everyone around her feel positive and happy, just like she is. It's no wonder she's been so successful.

Physically, Kim is freakily symmetrical. Is it fair to say hers is one of the prettiest faces I've worked on? No, it's not. I've worked with too many gorgeous women, all beautifully unique. But I can say Kim is the prettiest Armenian woman I've transformed. (Okay, she's also my first.) She can wear any look, so I decided to take her from Hollywood celebrity to fashion model. It's not every day that she gets to be so pa-pow! So, why not? After all, she can rival any supermodel, complete with curves that make her that much more luscious.

Physically, Kim is freakily SYMMETRICAL.

Kim on Scott, Business, and Beauty

When I got the call to work with Scott, obviously it felt like such a privilege. I had heard so much about him, and I've always wanted to work with him. The whole day was just magic, a real pleasure. I love all types of makeup and learning different techniques. I've always said that if I weren't doing what I'm doing now I'd probably be a makeup artist because I love experimenting with makeup. I probably have more makeup at home than makeup artists do! I was anxious to see what Scott would do differently. I told him, "Do whatever you want," and he completely transformed my face! Scott's a genius—just brilliant—at what he does. His technique of applying makeup is completely different from anything I've ever seen before. His makeup line is amazing too, and I got to take some of it home—a real bonus. I've been using it ever since!

I've always been into fashion and beauty, and I've always had a very strong business sense. I've worked since I was in high school, figuring out one business after another. My dad was a lawyer, so growing up, we signed contracts for everything—mini contracts he would prepare for us. So, when I got my first car, he made me sign a contract that stated I was responsible for its upkeep, washing it once a week, and so on; and if I ever damaged it, I would have to pay for the repairs. When I eventually did damage my car—a little rear-end accident when I was 16 years old—I had to pay for the repairs, so I got a job working in a clothing store.

I also worked in my dad's law office for seven years and was always doing these little deals with him. I remember one time when these Manolo Blahnik Timberland-looking boots came out on eBay. They were priced at £350 a pair, and I told my dad, "Dad, I know the girl at Manolo Blahnik. I can get a hook-up. I want to get eight to ten pairs of these shoes. Can I

put it on your credit card?" He was like, "You're crazy, what are you doing?!" And I said, "Please trust me, I'll pay you back with interest." He finally agreed, kind of like, "Okay, I want to see what little business my daughter has going on." So, I bought these boots, and I talked the girl into giving me X number of pairs. There was this crazy waiting list, and no one could get them. Since I got them before anyone else, I put them up on eBay and sold each pair for £1,250. I paid my dad his money back within two weeks, with interest.

Then I started a closet company where I would organise people's closets, kind of a combination of organiser, personal stylist, and personal shopper. So, whatever the person didn't want I would sell for them on eBay. My clients were Nicole Richie and Paris Hilton, people like that, so it was fun.

I have several things going now: my own perfume, a workout DVD, and a shoe line called ShoeDazzle.com, which basically offers a person their own shoe stylist who helps pick out a pair of shoes.

I also spend time working with The Dream Foundation, an organization that grants wishes to terminally ill adults. This is a cause that's very close to my heart. I attend events, and sometimes I help to fulfill a person's dream. For example, an adult might have a last wish to meet a celebrity or go to a sporting event. There was one girl who just wanted to get her hair and makeup done and spend the day with me, so that's what we did: spent the day together. We had an amazing time. She wrote me a beautiful letter before she died, which was very fulfilling for me too.

People ask whether I find it depressing. I don't, although there can be a huge element of sadness. My dad obviously passed away as an adult, and if he were to have a last wish, I would've liked to have granted that for him. So, now I'm helping other people by helping them ease their last few months or weeks. Overall, I'd say it's more heartwarming than depressing. I just always try to look at the positive side of things: A person got his or her final wish granted, and I was able to help with that.

Staying positive and feeling good is important in life and is a huge part of feeling beautiful. I'm definitely an advocate of taking care of oneself when it comes to beauty. I blog about it all the time. I am not a big drinker, and I definitely go to lots of events. But I'm extremely focused, and I sleep. Sleep is so important and is probably the main reason why I have so much energy. I also make sure I exercise every day, drink water, and take care of myself in general. I work out

in the morning—you just have to make time for it. I think it's really about making a commitment to yourself.

It's also important not to pay too much attention to what's in the magazines, their beauty standards, because there are so many different kinds of beauty. I'm very curvy, not your stick-skinny Hollywood girl, and I'll never be that tall, skinny supermodel; that's just not me. But I've learned to embrace who I am, embrace my shape. Everyone should try to do what they can to work with what they've got. I think if everyone did that, they'd be a lot happier. Why waste all that time worrying about things you can't change? I believe everyone can be happy, but you've got to do what it takes to look your best. Then you'll feel your best. That's just how it works!

Our deepest fear is not
that we are inadequate.
Our deepest fear is that
we are powerful beyond measure.
It is our light, not our darkness,
that most frightens us.
We ask ourselves, who am I to be brilliant,
gorgeous, talented, and fabulous?
Actually, who are you not to be?

—Nelson Mandela

From Scott

The first time I laid eyes on Jennifer Lopez she was wearing a pair of jeans, high heels, a blue leather jacket, a turtleneck, and a pair of blue aviators. Her hair was pulled back and she was wearing no makeup. She looked radiant.

Up to this point, I had seen Jennifer with a certain "look." She was always made up to project structure, with lots of contour and shading. But for this photo shoot, I wanted her to look like herself, just the best possible version of that. She sat down and I began a series of beauty rituals to tap into her essence and to release what was already there but was waiting to come out. Halfway through our session, Jennifer started to radiate. She began to notice her reflection in the mirror. The results were extraordinary.

That same day Jennifer asked me to do her makeup for her *J.Lo* album cover, and we've been working together ever since. For the first two years, we maintained a monochromatic look, establishing her as a glowing bronze beauty. I created an entire movement from working with J. Lo, and suddenly, being the fashion icon that she is, bronze skin, beige lips, and a monochromatic palette was the new look. Jennifer became recognized as one of the most beautiful women in the world.

Jennifer connected with her inner beauty. And I believe every woman has the potential to do the same. Jennifer and I have taught each other many things. She's been a positive presence in my life ever since the day we met. I will always be grateful for that.

Scott

About the Author

Scott Barnes is a celebrated makeup artist and innovator within the cosmetics industry.

He arrived in New York City in 1984 determined to fulfill his dream as a fine-arts painter. After attending New York's prestigious Parsons School of Design, Scott began assisting on fashion photography shoots and quickly became one of the most sought after makeup artists in the industry.

International beauty guru Shu Uemura selected Scott to revamp his Atelier Made line, which became a huge success within the fashion industry and among celebrities. Following his success at Shu Uemura, Scott launched his own twenty-one-piece colour cosmetic line, Scott Barnes Cosmetics, on QVC in April 2004. Five months later, Scott introduced 130 products at Holt Renfrew, in Canada, Saks Fifth Avenue, in the U.S., and other high-end specialty boutiques. A year later, the collection launched in Europe and Australia and became an overnight success for which *Women's Wear Daily* named Scott the "Newcomer of the Year." He was also a finalist for the Fashion Group International's "Rising Star" award.

Scott Barnes has worked with world-renowned photographers, including Patrick Demarchelier, Scavullo, Gilles Bensimon, Tony Duran, Peter Lindbergh, Annie Leibovitz, Ruven Afanador, and Mark Seliger with his work gracing the covers of such leading magazines as *Elle*, *Harper's Bazaar*, *InStyle*, *Vanity Fair*, *Rolling Stone*, and *Marie Claire*. Scott has also appeared on television programmes, such as *The Oprah Winfrey Show*.

Although Scott has worked with a variety of Hollywood talent over the years, including Kate Hudson, Beyonce, Gwyneth Paltrow, and Celine Dion, it's his work with Jennifer Lopez that birthed the new monochromatic look featuring bronzed skin and pale lips. Described as "The Glow," this signature look became known as "lit from within" and helped launch Scott's best-selling beauty product, Body Bling bronzer.

In addition to numerous ad campaigns and music videos, Scott's work on set includes such films as *El Cantante*, which earned him Oscar consideration. Scott was also responsible for Jennifer Lopez's memorable Cinderella moments in *Maid in Manhattan*.

Acknowledgments

Making this book has been a huge undertaking and a testament to my faith. I would like to thank God for his steadfast love, thank you!

I would like to thank the following people for all their hard work and dedication:

Fair Winds Press for the opportunity and belief in this book. Will Kiester, Rosalind Wanke, and Sylvia McArdle, thank you for making this a great experience. I would like to thank David D'Amico, you were a godsend, I would love to do it again. Lydia Latrowski, you keep me looking smooth. Jennifer Lopez and Mark Anthony, Simon Fields, Debbie Izzard, Celine Dion. Karl Simone, who has always been a great friend and a wonderful photographer. Jocelyn Goldstein, for her fly sense of style. Chuck "Chuckie Love" Amos, make it bigger, wilder, and sexier! Dana Benningfield, you took all my words and made sense of them, Phew...! Lorraine Schwartz, for your stunning jewelry. Lenny and Antonia Trimarchi, your jewelry "rocks." Larry Schatz, for your constant belief in me, what can I say, I am blessed to have you on my side. Milk Studios, for a beautiful workspace to create beauty. Oscar Reyes and Dani Bongiorno. Kim Kardashian, Judith Light, Mariska Hargitay, and Kat Deluna. Dr. Jessica Wu, I told you!!! Dr. Eva Cwynar, Maureen and Marley Kornowa, thank you for sharing your story with us, it means the world to me. Diane Von Furstenberg, Michael Kors, Catherine Malandrino, Marc Jacobs, and everyone else who assisted me on these shoots. And my Family, especially my Godmother, Aunt Jackie, whose unwavering support pushed me to be my best.